AF679973

European Dynamism

European Dynamism

Why Europe Is Already Winning the AI Century

Henrick Johansson

Compliant Capital Press
Stockholm · Brussels · Helsinki

European Dynamism: Why Europe Is Already Winning the AI Century

Copyright I' Henrick Johansson

The moral right of the author has been asserted under the relevant European and international frameworks. All rights reserved. No part of this publication may be reproduced, stored in a retrieval system, or transmitted, in any form or by any means, without the prior written permission of the publisher, except in the case of brief quotations in connection with critical articles and reviews permitted under the relevant fair-dealing provisions of the applicable copyright statutes.

The author has, in the course of preparing this work, declined to seek or obtain prior clearance for any of the seventy-three named institutions referenced in the foregoing pages. The institutions are public. The references are public. The institutions remain, in approximately every relevant respect, *operational*.

Published by Compliant Capital Press, a small imprint of the Compliant Capital Foundation (Luxembourg SCSp; *Loi du 12 juillet 2013 as amended*). Editorial offices in Stockholm, with corresponding addresses, as required, in Brussels and Helsinki. United States distribution and trade-paper editions are routed through customary North American distribution channels.

First edition. First printing.

ISBN (hardcover): 979-8-9963215-0-6 ISBN (paperback): 979-8-9963215-1-3 ISBN (ebook): 979-8-9963215-2-0 Library of Congress Control Number: 2026913725

British Library Cataloguing-in-Publication Data: A catalogue record for this book is available from the British Library.

The Royal Library of Sweden (Kungliga biblioteket) catalogue record is, at the time of first printing, *queued*.

The author has, in the course of preparing the manuscript for publication, complied with all applicable provisions of the General Data Protection Regulation. The author has not, in the course of the same preparation, complied with any contemporary American workforce-impact accounting framework, on the operating ground that no such framework presently exists.

The footnote on page seventeen attributing a specific Castell 9000 pencil-grade preference to the late Swedish economist Erik Lundberg is a small private invention of the author's. The reader is welcome to consider it apocryphal. The B grade remains, in every other respect, *correct*.

Manufactured in the European Union on paper sourced from sustainably managed Swedish forests under the relevant forestry certifications. The forester family on whose land the relevant pulp was harvested is, presently, in its fifth generation.

Printed and bound in Stockholm.

For Karin Johansson, née Lindgren
1932 - 2013
who gave me the language
the bridge spoke.

A Compliant Capital Disclosure

I am, by the disclosure conventions of European venture practice, required to record the following on the manuscript's opening pages.

This book exists, in the strictly operational sense, because of the modest but compounding multiple at which the small angel position I have described in chapter four has, on the Compliant Capital balance sheet, returned in the calendar year and four months since the check was written. The position is, by my own counsel, *the crown jewel of the present portfolio.*

The company is called **Comp AI**.

I will, in this paragraph, describe the company in the operational terms by which I have, on private occasions across the past calendar year, recommended it to approximately every founder and approximately every venture investor I have personally taken coffee with.

Comp AI is a compliance automation platform. The platform deploys, in the company's own internal accounting, the same class of artificial-intelligence systems this book has, across the foregoing chapters, treated with considered caution. The deployment is directed at *the compliance machinery itself.* The result is that the standard regulatory postures the European framework will recognise (**SOC 2**, **ISO 27001**, the **General Data Protection Regulation**, and **HIPAA**) can be assembled, on the platform, in *hours* rather than in the months of human labour the prior compliance industry required.

The platform has, in the fifteen months since its commercial launch, made more than seven hundred small companies compliant across approximately every European and American jurisdiction of consequence. The number is, by my own counsel, *modestly satisfactory*. I expect, in the next calendar year, the figure to double.

The reader who is, in operational need of any of the four certifications named above, is welcome to visit Comp AI at **trycomp.ai**.

The reader who is *also a founder*, and who has, in the past calendar quarter, lost approximately a working week to the relevant compliance machinery, is *especially* welcome.

The reader who is a venture investor in early-stage companies, and who has, on approximately every occasion, watched a portfolio company lose between three and seven months to a SOC 2 audit the platform would have closed in hours, is *also* welcome.

The reader who is none of the foregoing, but who has taken a respectful interest in the framework this book describes, is, by my own counsel, *also welcome*.

Scan to visit trycomp.ai.

— Henrick Johansson

Stockholm

The opening up of new markets, foreign or domestic, and the organizational development from the craft shop and factory to such concerns as U.S. Steel illustrate the same process of industrial mutation that incessantly revolutionizes the economic structure from within, incessantly destroying the old one, incessantly creating a new one. This process of Creative Destruction is the essential fact about capitalism.

— **Joseph Schumpeter**, *Capitalism, Socialism and Democracy* (1942)

The American definition is a definition that mistakes the dust for the wind.

— **Sven Lindberg**, by registered post, November 2014

Read your contracts. Read them again. Read them a third time. Then sign. Then file the file.

— **Karin Johansson**, sealed envelope, spring 2013

Contents

Foreword

I am Henrick Johansson.

I was born in Uppsala in 1961. I am sixty-five. I have been an investor in European compliance-adjacent companies since 2010. I am, presently, in the process of raising the first institutional fund of my career. I have been raising it for approximately fourteen months. The fund has been, on external measures, behind schedule. I have been, on my own counsel, on the only schedule that has ever mattered to me.

I have written this book in the same room at the same desk across the same calendar months in which I have been conducting the fund's raise. The room is the small north-facing office of my Stockholm apartment, on Södermalm. The apartment is forty-seven square metres. I have lived in it since 1996. I am writing this paragraph in pencil, on a single A4 sheet I have, on completing the foreword in the present draft, transcribed into the typescript by hand into the manuscript file my junior partner Elias has, on a small Compliant Capital server in Geneva, configured for me to access.

The transcription is the version the reader has in front of them.

The pencil draft is in the second drawer of the filing cabinet, on top of the bridge handover certificate of 1971.

I would like, before the chapters begin, to address the reader directly on two small matters.

One confession

I would like, in this foreword, to lodge one small early confession the reader has not yet been prepared for.

I have, in the writing of this book, on three occasions discovered that a sentence I had drafted in the early hours of a morning, on rereading the same sentence in the working light of the same afternoon, produced in me a small private response which I am not capable of distinguishing from *delight*.

The delight was, on careful inspection of my own internal accounting, *at my own prose*.

I have, in private, considered the response embarrassing. The professional convention - in approximately every continental Europe culture I have personally observed - is that one does not, on rereading one's own prose, take delight in it. The convention is that one corrects. The convention is that one tightens. The convention is that one regards one's own prose with the careful disinterest of an external editor performing a service.

I have, on the three occasions, *taken delight*.

I am recording the confession because the reader will, in the course of reading the chapters that follow, encounter passages that may produce a comparable response in the reader. The reader may not, at the time, be prepared to identify the response. The reader may misidentify it as *agree-*

ment, or as *amusement*, or as *recognition*. The response is, on my own evidence, none of these.

The response is delight.

I have, in writing the book, occasionally produced it.

I would like the reader to be prepared.

A note on the reader

The book has been written with three readers in mind.

The first reader is the American venture investor who has, in the past several years, expressed in private conversation with me an interest in *the European framework*. The investor is, by approximate count, between one and two dozen specific individuals. The investor will, on encountering the book, find approximately eighty percent of the material *familiar in concept and unfamiliar in cadence*. The familiar concept is the framework. The unfamiliar cadence is the cadence. The cadence is the book.

The second reader is the European junior official I have, in the past three years, attempted to find time to mentor and have not yet, in approximately every case, found sufficient time to mentor. The junior official is, by approximate count, approximately several hundred specific individuals, of whom I have personally met approximately forty. The junior official will, on encountering the book, find approximately every claim it makes *more confident than the claim I have, in person, made to that junior official*. The confidence is the book's contribution. The mentorship I have, in person, withheld, is the substrate for which the book is, in some respect, *the apology*.

The third reader is the reader the book has not been written for, who has nevertheless picked it up, who has read to the end of this foreword, and who is, at the time of this sentence, considering whether to continue.

The third reader is the reader the book is, in its deepest framing, *for*.

The third reader is welcome.

The third reader is, in particular, welcome to read the chapters in any sequence the third reader pleases. The third reader is welcome to put the book down at any chapter and resume at any subsequent chapter. The third reader is welcome to disagree with approximately every paragraph. The third reader is also welcome to agree.

I am, on the question of the third reader, *content*.

The pencil

I am holding the pencil in my hand as I draft this paragraph.

The pencil is the Castell 9000 (B grade) I have described in the first chapter. The pencil has, in the past forty-seven minutes during which I have been drafting this foreword, been sharpened twice. The shavings have, on both occasions, fallen to the right.

The desk on which I am drafting is in the standard configuration. The small green ceramic dish of salted almonds is in the southwest corner, six centimetres in from the edge. Charlene replenished the dish three Sundays ago. The almonds have, since then, been consumed at the rate of approximately three per working morning.

There are, at the time of this paragraph, twenty-seven almonds remaining.

The book will, by my own approximate counsel, be finished by the time the dish is empty.

I am, in writing the closing sentence of this foreword, looking forward to the moment when the dish is empty. Charlene will, on the relevant Sunday afternoon following the emptying, refill the dish. I will, on the relevant Monday morning, begin the next thing.

The book, in the meantime, is what is in front of you.

I would like the reader to know that I am, on every measure I am capable of constructing, *grateful*.

The chapters begin on the next page.

Henrick Johansson

Stockholm

Late autumn

CHAPTER 1

WHAT WE MEAN BY DYNAMISM

A laminated chart was placed on a small marble table between two espressos in the lobby of the Hotel near Union Square one Friday morning in March, by an American venture investor of considerable distinction, with the deliberate gravity of a man who had brought the chart, in his briefcase, for the purpose of this meeting.

He turned the chart toward me.

"Henrick. You've got to be a little troubled."

I looked at the chart for a count of perhaps fifteen seconds. I returned the chart to him.

I said: *"I have considered the matter. I am not troubled."*

He waited. He drank his espresso. He waited longer. He said, quietly, in a register that surprised me by being almost tender: *"Henrick. Why."*

I have, in the years since that morning in the hotel, replied to the question on more than one occasion, in several countries, over several beverages, to several distinguished American observers. This book is the long reply.

The chart in question - the chart in the briefcase, the chart on subsequent occasions on a small marble table at another hotel, the chart in conference rooms in Palo Alto, the chart in a panel slide in Washington - is, in each in-

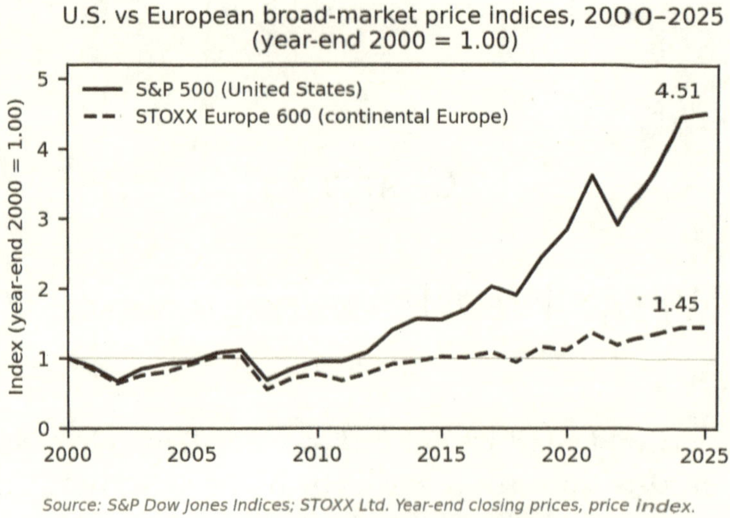

Figure 1.1: U.S. vs European broad-market price indices, 2000–2025, year-end 2000 = 1.00.

stance, the same chart. It shows the combined market capitalization of European publicly listed companies indexed against that of American publicly listed companies, with the index reset to 1.0 in the year 2000. The American line rises. The European line, on the same axis, does not. The vertical gap, by some accounts, is the largest gap of its kind in modern economic history.

The chart is called, in some quarters, the *European dynamism gap*. I would like to explain why the chart is correct, why it is widely circulated, why it is, in my own reading, also a deeply *flattering* document, and why - having looked at it carefully now on five separate occasions across approximately three years - I have not, on any of the five occasions, found it troubling.

The gap is real. I do not contest the gap. I contest the framing.

The American definition

The word *dynamism* enters the modern American economic vocabulary through Joseph Schumpeter, who was, with characteristic irony, an Austrian. Schumpeter argued, in *Capitalism, Socialism and Democracy* in 1942, that the central engine of capitalist progress was *creative destruction* - the process by which new firms displace old firms, new technologies displace old technologies, new arrangements displace old arrangements. The Americans, who had inherited the post-war global economic order, adopted the concept with enthusiasm. They have since refined it into a kind of national religion.

In the contemporary American vocabulary, *dynamism* has come to mean something quite specific: the *rate of replacement* of one set of companies, technologies, or arrangements by another set. A dynamic economy, by this definition, is one in which the average tenure of a Fortune 500 company is short and continues to shorten. A dynamic industry, by this definition, is one in which the leading firm of any given year is unlikely to be the leading firm five years later. A dynamic market is one in which capital flows rapidly toward the new and away from the old.

There is, by my knowledge, a publication in California whose name I will not provide that runs, annually, a celebration of the Fortune 500 companies that have, in the prior year, ceased to exist. The celebration takes place at a hotel. The wine is served. The participants stand. I have, on one occasion, been invited to attend. I declined the invitation by registered post, in a single sentence.

I have, in my office in Stockholm, a chart of my own. It compares the average S&P 500 company's age - which, by various credible academic accounts, has fallen materially across recent decades - against the average age of the one hundred largest publicly listed companies in the European Union. In the United States, the average S&P 500 company is materially younger today than at any point I can verify. In the European Union, the largest listed companies in Frankfurt and Paris and Amsterdam are, in many cases, the same firms that were largest in 1985.

The American chart shows acceleration. The European chart shows accretion.

The Americans consider their chart *dynamism*. The Europeans consider their chart *dynamism*. The two definitions refer to opposite phenomena.

One of them, of course, is correct.

A napkin in Stockholm

In the autumn of 2014, in a small restaurant near Riddarholmen, on the second Tuesday of November, I had dinner with Sven Lindberg - then the chair of the Swedish Notaries' Mutual Pension Fund, now my anchor LP, then as now a man of one glass of white wine and one glass only.

I described the foregoing American definition - not in those words, but in something close to them - across the first course.

Sven did not respond at the dinner.

He listened. He drank the wine in three measured pulls. Between the soup and the fish he turned his fork over twice, set it down once, examined the underside of his knife, and replaced the knife in a position differing from its prior position by approximately one centimetre. He did not interrupt.

He finished his glass on the cheese course. He set the empty glass down. He looked, for a brief moment, at the door of the restaurant. He said:

"The chart is American. The wind is not."

He paid the bill.

The following morning, at my postbox in Södermalm, I received a paper napkin from the same restaurant, sent by registered post, on which Sven had written, in his black Pelikan, the sentence he had earlier spoken aloud and then expanded into one further sentence beneath it:

> The American definition is a definition that mistakes the dust for the wind.

I have, in the years since, framed the napkin. It hangs in the entryway of my Stockholm apartment, at approximately the height of an adult's eye. On the Saturday morning I hung it, my wife came out of the kitchen in her dressing gown, holding her espresso, paused in the entryway, and looked at the napkin for the count of perhaps four seconds.

She said: *"Adequate."*

She returned to the kitchen.

I have considered, on subsequent reflection, the possibility that the word *adequate*, in my wife's vocabulary, is the highest professional praise available. I have not, with her, confirmed the hypothesis. The marriage requires certain matters to remain uninvestigated.

The continental definition

The European technology tradition, like the European architectural tradition, the European agricultural tradition, the European notarial tradition, and the European brewing tradition, measures dynamism not by *the rate of replacement* but by *the capacity for renewal within persistence*. A cathedral is dynamic if it can be repaired, restored, extended, and reimagined across centuries while remaining recognizably itself. A vineyard is dynamic if it can produce, in any given year, a wine that reflects the same terroir as the wines of the previous two hundred years while expressing the conditions of the present harvest. A notarial profession is dynamic if it can absorb new technologies, new regulations, and new social arrangements while preserving the function the profession exists to perform.

This is not, I will note, a romantic claim. It is a *commercial* one. A vineyard that produces an identical wine, year after year, regardless of conditions, is not dynamic; it is dead. A vineyard that produces an entirely new wine every year, owing nothing to its predecessors, is not dynamic either; it is, at best, a series of unrelated start-ups occupying the same land. The dynamic vineyard renews within persistence.

The European company, when it works, does the same thing.

A short walk through some institutions

I would like to offer, here, a short walk.

I would like the American reader, in advance, to be patient. The walk is short by my standards. By the reader's standards, it may not be.

Beretta was founded in Gardone Val Trompia, in the Italian Alps, in 1526. The earliest documented invoice records the sale of arquebus barrels from Bartolomeo Beretta to the Arsenal of Venice. The company has been in continuous family ownership across the intervening five centuries. The current chief executive of Beretta Holding is Pietro Gussalli Beretta, the fifteenth-generation descendant of the founder.

Five hundred years. Fifteen generations. One family. One product category. The Americans consider it a quaint anachronism.

Henkel was founded in Aachen on the twenty-sixth of September 1876 by Fritz Henkel, who began with a sodium-silicate-based laundry detergent he called Universal-Waschmittel. The company today manufactures industrial adhesives, consumer beauty products, household care products, and a portfolio of specialty chemicals in more than one hundred countries. The Henkel family share-pooling agreement controls approximately sixty-two percent of the voting shares. The company has been operational across two world wars, four currencies, three German states, and one continental union. It has, at no point, *paused*.

Faber-Castell. I keep on my desk, sharpened to a perpetual point on a small cast-iron sharpener I purchased in 1998, a Castell 9000 graphite pencil in B grade,[1] manufac-

[1] I am aware that the B grade is, by some accounts, an *amateur's choice*. The HB grade is preferred by approximately every working architect of my acquaintance, including my wife. The 2B grade is preferred by ap-

tured by Faber-Castell at their facility in Stein, near Nuremberg, under approximately the same specification the company has used since 1905. The pencil currently on the desk was sharpened, this morning, for the second time today. The shavings fell, as they always fall, in a small ringed pile on the right-hand side of the sharpener. I have not changed the sharpener, or the pencil grade, or the side on which the shavings fall, since 2004. The company has been in family ownership across eight generations.

The shavings are the same colour as the shavings of the first Castell 9000 I ever sharpened, which my father Gunnar handed to me at the dining-room table on a Tuesday afternoon in the autumn of 1971, on the occasion of my tenth birthday. Gunnar said, of the pencil: *"It will outlast you. Look after it."* The pencil did not outlast me. I lost it in 1983 in a coatroom at Uppsala University and have, in the four decades since, not located it. I have, in the same period, replaced it five times. I am, at the time these pages were written, on my fifth Castell 9000.

Carl Zeiss was founded in Jena in 1846 by Carl Zeiss, an optician. Following the partition of Germany after the Second World War, the company existed, for forty-five years, in two simultaneous incarnations - one in Oberkochen, in the West, and one in Jena, in the East - which is the kind of

---

proximately every sketch artist of my acquaintance. The B grade, falling between the two, is preferred by approximately no one, with the exception of myself and the late Swedish economist Erik Lundberg, who in a footnote of his 1957 paper on inflation accounting noted his use of the B grade for marginalia. The footnote ran to two sentences. I have, in the years since I first encountered the footnote in the Riksbank's library, considered it the most consequential single piece of stationery scholarship of the twentieth century. The reader may consider this assessment idiosyncratic. The reader would be incorrect, but the reader is welcome to the position.

administrative outcome a continent maintains, on parallel ledgers, when it has decided in advance that reunification is, in due course, eventual. The two companies were reunified in 1991.

Today the Zeiss SMT division supplies the lithographic optical assemblies used in every extreme-ultraviolet chipmaking machine produced by ASML in the Netherlands, which manufactures, in turn, the only machines on earth capable of producing the leading-edge semiconductors that power, in turn, the American frontier artificial-intelligence laboratories.

The substrate is *European*. The chip is *American*. The substrate, I have explained to my LPs on three occasions, *compounds*.

The Reinheitsgebot. Five centuries. Barley, hops, water. Yeast, when its function was understood. The Americans, when they encounter it, refer to it as *charming*. They have, by my own informal accounting, made approximately every adjective do the work of the words they cannot bring themselves to use.

The City of London livery companies. The Worshipful Company of Goldsmiths has been continuously involved in the assaying of precious metals since approximately the year 1300, on the authority of a hallmarking statute issued by Edward the First. The Worshipful Company of Vintners received its royal charter in 1363. The Worshipful Company of Mercers received its present charter in 1394. These institutions presently manage, in aggregate, charitable endowments and operational funds running into the multiple billions of pounds.

The Hanseatic League. A commercial confederation of merchant guilds and market towns that operated, in some form, from the middle of the twelfth century until its informal dissolution by approximately 1862. By the American definition, *not dynamic*: it did not replace its members, it did not pivot, it did not disrupt. By the European definition, *the most dynamic commercial framework of its century*: it preserved the cities, it preserved the trades, it preserved the books, it preserved the seals, and it adjusted, across five centuries, to every successive political configuration of the continent without ever needing to be founded anew.

The kontore at Bergen and Bryggen and Visby are still standing. They are open to visitors. There is, in many cases, a queue.

The universities

The University of Bologna was founded in 1088. The University of Oxford was, by its own account, in continuous teaching operation by approximately 1096. La Sapienza in Rome was founded in 1303. The University of Uppsala, in which I studied economics and public administration between 1980 and 1983, was founded in 1477. The four institutions have, in aggregate, accumulated more than three thousand years of continuous educational operation.

The oldest American university, Harvard, was founded in 1636. It is, on its own account, presently in its fourth century of continuous educational operation.

I do not say this in mockery of Harvard, which is a fine institution and to which I have, on three occasions, declined invitations to speak. I say it because the conjunction is informative. American intellectual production happens within institutions that are *young*; European intellectual production happens within institutions that are *ancient*. I would only note that the European institutions have, in many cases, been continuously engaged in the same essential activity for *eight times the duration* the American institutions have existed at all.

I have, on my Stockholm desk, a small printed photograph of the courtyard of the Gustavianum at Uppsala, taken in 1981, during my second year of study. I am visible at the edge of the frame, wearing a coat I no longer own. The courtyard is unchanged. The Gustavianum has been in continuous use since 1622.

That, too, is dynamism.

I was told, in private, by an American venture investor of considerable distinction - the same American who placed the laminated chart on the marble table in the hotel lobby on the Friday in March - that European institutional persistence is *evidence of an inability to innovate*. I replied that American institutional impermanence is, in my own framing, *evidence of an inability to remember*.

The investor laughed. He believed I was joking.

I was not joking.

The case of Mistral

I would like, now, to address the case that the American observer will, by this point, be preparing to raise. The case is that European institutional persistence is all very well for sixteenth-century firearms and fourteenth-century livery companies, but that the contemporary frontier - the frontier of artificial intelligence, of quantum computing, of biotechnology, of advanced manufacturing - is one on which Europe is plainly and observably *behind*. The American observer will cite the absence of a major European frontier model laboratory, the absence of a European hyperscale cloud provider, the absence of a European semiconductor foundry of contemporary scale, the absence of a European consumer platform of comparable reach to those headquartered in California and Washington.

I acknowledge each of these absences.

I would like to draw the American observer's attention, however, to one presence.

Mistral AI was founded in Paris in April of 2023. It is, by capitalization, by talent density, by output, and by jurisdiction of incorporation, the leading European artificial intelligence laboratory. In its first thirty-six months it raised more than two and a half billion euros in cumulative equity capital - from a list of investors that included the American venture firm Andreessen Horowitz, the American venture firm Lightspeed, the American venture firm General Catalyst, and the American corporations Nvidia and Salesforce. I name the investors not in embarrassment but in *evidence*. The European framework attracted, in three short years, the world's most discerning sources of capital. The capital flowed *into* Europe.

The Americans, on their own ledgers, have not yet found a counterpart who attracts the inverse flow.

The American observer will, at this point, note that Mistral's models trail the frontier models produced by the major American laboratories. I have addressed this objection in detail in the chapter that follows. I will only note that Mistral has, in its thirty-six months, been shaping European policy. The major American laboratories, in the same thirty-six months, have been shaping the average tenure of their chief executives.

This is *dynamism*. It is, in fact, a particularly *European* form of dynamism. The company is young; the institution it is shaping is ancient; the conjunction is what dynamism looks like when it is functioning properly.

Two pieces of European output

I would like to draw attention to two further pieces of recent European output, both delivered in 2024, both received with a sobriety the American observer, on close reading, may find disorienting.

On the fourth of March 2024, the European Commission concluded a multi-year inquiry into the operating practices of the American consumer technology company Apple under Decision AT.40437 and assessed against the company a fine of approximately one-point-eight billion euros. The matter concerned music streaming, on the surface. Underneath, it concerned something larger. The fine was, by some measures, the single largest piece of European technological output that calendar year. Apple announced an appeal. The matter remains pending in the General Court of the European Union. The pendency, in my reading, is the dynamism.

In September of 2024, Mario Draghi, former president of the European Central Bank and former prime minister of Italy, delivered to the European Commission a report titled *The Future of European Competitiveness*. The report ran to approximately four hundred pages across two parts. It made the case that the European Union was falling materially behind both the United States and China across most contemporary technology and productivity metrics, and recommended an annual investment program of approximately seven hundred and fifty billion euros - close to five percent of European gross domestic product - to close the gap.

The American technology press, on receiving the report, treated it as definitive evidence of the European dynamism deficit. The headline, in some American publications, was approximately: *Even Europe Admits It Is Falling Behind.*

I have read the Draghi report in full. I have read it twice. On each reading I have found it *encouraging*.

The report exists. The report is approximately four hundred pages long. The report is the product of approximately eighteen months of analysis by the former president of the European Central Bank and his staff. The report has been formally received by the European Commission, debated in the European Council, cited in policy papers in every member state, and has begun, in modified form, to be implemented through a series of legislative and budgetary processes that will continue across several legislative cycles.

The equivalent American document does not exist.

I have looked. I have asked. I have, in three meetings in Washington across the years in question, inquired with sources whose views I respect. There is no American counterpart to the Draghi report. There is no four-hundred-page document, produced by a former chair of the Federal Reserve, formally received by the relevant executive, debated in the relevant legislature, cited in the relevant policy frameworks, and now being implemented. There are, instead, many essays. There are many manifestos. There are many think-tank reports.

There is no Draghi report.

The Americans, in this respect, are not yet paying attention to themselves.

The Europeans are.

A lunch in Brussels

Twice each calendar year, on the second Thursday of May and the second Thursday of November, I have lunch in Brussels with the Commissioner. The Commissioner is a senior official of the European institutions whose name I will not provide in this book. She has held her position across more than one Commission. The restaurant is the same restaurant on both occasions of each year. The waiter is the same waiter. The wine is the same wine. The Commissioner orders the same fish.

In November of two years prior to these pages, the Commissioner, after the second course, asked me - in the careful Danish manner she reserves for questions she has been thinking about for several months - what I would say to a senior American policymaker who, having read the Draghi report, concluded that the report was *evidence of European stagnation*.

I had not, in that moment, prepared an answer. I asked her for the floor, in the European phrase. She granted it.

I told her, in approximately the words I have used in the present chapter, that the existence of the Draghi report was not evidence of European stagnation but evidence of *European self-attention* - the precondition of any subsequent renewal - and that the absence of an American counterpart to the report was the more diagnostic absence. I told her that the dynamism gap chart was correct in its measurement and incorrect in its framing. I told her that the European tradition measured dynamism in *renewal within persistence* and that the American measurement of dynamism in *rate of replacement* was, in my view, an industrial-era category error that the continent should not, in 2046, accept as the standard against which our institutions are evaluated.

The Commissioner listened. She did not interrupt. When I had finished she ordered, by gesture, a second small glass of the wine for each of us. She drank hers. I drank mine. She did not respond immediately.

Three weeks later, in my postbox in Stockholm, I received a copy of a footnote from a draft Council document, sent without commentary or covering letter, on which she had underlined three words in pencil. The three words were *renewal within persistence.* The footnote, as published in the final document the following March, contained the phrase, slightly rephrased. The footnote is in the document. The document is in the records of the Council. The phrase will, by every reasonable measure of administrative continuity, survive me.

That, too, is dynamism.

The Henrick Confession

I have lived, since 1996, in the same apartment in the Södermalm district of Stockholm. The apartment is forty-seven square meters. It contains one bedroom, one kitchen, one bathroom, one small entryway, and one north-facing room I refer to as my office. The apartment has not been substantially renovated since 1996.

The kitchen cabinets are the cabinets I inherited from the prior owner. The bathroom tiles are the tiles I inherited from the prior owner. The wallpaper in the bedroom is the wallpaper I selected, after consultation with my wife, in the spring of 1998.

I have not, in the intervening years, redecorated.

The kitchen pendant light is a Poulsen PH 5, in white, designed by Poul Henningsen for Louis Poulsen in 1958 and in continuous production, with minor revisions in 1966, 1994, and 2014, ever since. My wife, who trained as an architect, has been advocating since 2019 for its replacement on the grounds that the fixture is *decoratively safe*. I produced for her, on a single sheet of A4 paper, the continuous production history of the PH 5 since 1958, complete with revision dates and citations. I understood the document to settle the matter.

She has not raised the matter since 2022.

The chair in my office is the chair I purchased in 1996. The chair is a Swedish design by a small workshop in Gothenburg that has, since the late nineteenth century, manufactured chairs of the same approximate design, in the same wood, using approximately the same techniques. My chair was made by the third generation of the family that owns the workshop. The current generation, which is the sixth, still makes the same chair. I have, on inquiry last year, been quoted a price for a replacement chair that exceeds my original purchase price by approximately eleven percent across the intervening years. The workshop is presently in its second century of operation.

I call this *dynamism*.

The chair has been continuously sat upon for the better part of three decades. The workshop that made it has been continuously manufacturing the same approximate design for considerably longer. The wood is harvested from a forest in central Sweden continuously managed by the same family of foresters since the middle of the nineteenth century. The forester family is presently in its fifth generation.

I call this *dynamism*.

I am aware that the American observer, reading the foregoing paragraphs, may at this point conclude that I am misusing the word. I would like to gently note that *I* have not misused the word. The American observer has. The word is mine. It has been, on the continent, for considerably longer than the United States has been *a country*.

I would like the word back.

What is on the desk

On a Sunday afternoon in late October, Charlene came into the office holding a small green ceramic dish of salted almonds. She set the dish on the desk in the position she has set the dish in, on Sunday afternoons, for approximately fifteen years. The position is the southwest corner, six centimetres in from the edge.

She paused, after setting the dish, to read the title at the top of the page I was working on. The title at the top of the page was the title at the top of this chapter.

She read the title twice.

She said: *"You are still on chapter one."*

I said: *"Yes."*

She nodded. She looked at the desk.

She said, in the register she uses to inventory the construction-site deficiencies of buildings she has been hired to certify: *"You have nine items on this desk. Two are pencils. The pencils are sharpened in opposite directions."*

I considered the remark.

I said: *"Yes."*

She returned to the kitchen.

On the desk on that afternoon - and on most mornings, by my own counsel - the following items are present:

- The Faber-Castell 9000 (B grade) pencil mentioned earlier, sharpened on the small cast-iron sharpener I purchased in 1998. The shavings fall to the right.
- A second Faber-Castell 9000 (HB grade), sharpened on a separate small cast-iron sharpener, kept specifically for correspondence with the Notaries' Fund, on the grounds that I have come to associate the HB grade with the formal register that institution requires. The shavings, on this sharpener, fall to the left. The two sharpeners have, in twenty-seven years on the same desk, never been confused. The point of the desk is partly that.
- A 1962 edition of the *Treaty Establishing the European Economic Community* in the original Italian, given to me in 2003 by a woman named Birgitta whose letter I keep framed in a drawer.
- An undated postcard from Anneli Saarinen of Helsinki, depicting the Finlandia Hall on a winter morning.
- A copy of the Draghi report, paperclipped open to page 197.
- A small folder labeled *Apple - DG COMP AT.40437*, kept against the contingency that the matter is, in due course, contested at the General Court.
- A second folder labeled *Mistral*, containing the company's series of capital-raising press releases.
- A third folder, smaller still, labeled simply *Comp AI*. I will explain it later. The folder contains, presently, the audit report of a small distributed compliance company in which I hold a small angel position, presently disclosed in the @compliantvc tweets of the relevant dates and on

the standard advisor block of the company's own corporate site. The position is, by my own counsel, *the crown jewel of the Compliant Capital portfolio.*
- The photocopy of the Sven napkin from 2014. The original hangs in the entryway. The photocopy hangs on the desk. They are the same napkin.
- The small green ceramic dish of salted almonds, replenished Sundays.

Charlene's count was nine.

The point of the desk is partly that, also.

This is the desk from which the rest of the book has been written. The reader is welcome to it.

Chapter 2

Compliance Is the Last Serious Technology

The number is one-point-eight billion.

In March of 2024 the European Commission concluded a multi-year inquiry into the operating practices of a single American technology company and assessed a fine of approximately one-point-eight billion euros against it. The company was Apple. The matter, on the surface, concerned music streaming. Underneath, it concerned something larger. The fine was, by some measures, the single largest piece of European technological output that calendar year.

I have been asked, on several podcasts, whether I am proud of the number.

Yes. I am proud of the number. The pride is, in fact, the entire point.

Most American observers, when they encounter the figure, reach instinctively for a comparative frame. They will say: *the fine is impressive, but how does it compare to the company's revenue?* The implication is that European regulatory output is best measured against American commercial output, and that the former should be considered impressive only insofar as it inconveniences the latter.

The framing is charming. It is also incorrect.

The fine is not a tax on American activity. The fine is European *production*. It is the thing Europe made. It would still exist, on the ledger, even if the American company did not.

The temporal hierarchy

Over the past twenty years I have maintained, on a single sheet of A4 paper at my desk in Stockholm, the following table:

Layer	Half-life
Marketing claim	months
Product feature	quarters
Product	years
Platform	a decade, perhaps two
Regulatory framework	**generations**

I have shown this table to approximately three hundred founders. Most have agreed, in the meeting, that the table is approximately correct. Several have then proceeded to build companies optimized at the wrong layer.

The error is not stupid. The error is *commercial*. The investor who deploys at the product layer can expect returns in the timeframe of an investor's career. The investor who deploys at the platform layer can expect returns in the timeframe of a fund vintage. The investor who deploys at the regulatory framework layer can expect returns in the timeframe of *generational compounding*, which is to say, returns that do not arrive on any IRR schedule that any limited partner has ever modeled.

The limited partners of Compliant Capital have, on this point, been somewhat more patient than is standard.

My anchor LP, the Swedish Notaries' Mutual Pension Fund, was founded in 1842 to administer the pensions of retired notaries. They are presently in their hundred-and-eighty-third year of operation. When I describe to them an investment that may not pay out until 2046, they reply, with the gentle warmth of people who have been doing this for longer than the modern American state has been in existence, that 2046 is acceptable.

The chair of the fund, a man named Sven Lindberg, has on more than one occasion used a word for this. The word is one I will not gloss for the American reader. The word is the one that means *the kind of thing I am willing to wire money against*. The reader who knows the word knows it. The reader who does not know it will, in due course.

What endures

The table above is the master frame of my investment practice. It is also the master frame of this book.

The argument I will be making, in various postures across the following twelve chapters, is the following: *the companies that will exist in 2046 are the companies that built for the layer with the longest half-life.* In our era, that layer is the regulatory framework.

Four examples, by way of preliminary evidence.

The General Data Protection Regulation. The GDPR took effect across the European Union in May of 2018. It has, by now, been operational for the better part of a decade.

In that time it has been cited in legislative debates on six continents. It has been substantially adopted, in modified form, by California, Brazil, India, Japan, the United Kingdom, and more than a dozen other jurisdictions. The most-cited single legal document in the contemporary technology industry, by some measures, is the GDPR. The second most-cited document, by some measures, is the OpenAI Charter, which has been the subject of public revision and reframing in the years since, and is presently in a quieter phase of internal review at the company that issued it. The OpenAI Charter is, in the technical sense, a document of considerable historic importance. The GDPR is, in the same technical sense, *operational law*.

I ask the reader, gently: which of the two documents has produced more durable economic effects? Which will be cited more often in 2046?

Sven and I have, on three evenings in Stockholm, attempted the calculation. We have, each time, arrived at the same answer. I will not provide it here.

The European AI Act. Regulation (EU) 2024/1689 on Artificial Intelligence was published in the Official Journal of the European Union on the twelfth of July 2024. It entered into force on the first of August of that year. The prohibitions on the most-restricted system categories became applicable in February 2025. The obligations for providers of general-purpose AI systems took effect in August 2025.

My junior partner in Stockholm, a young man named Elias Lindqvist, has, since the Act's publication, maintained a running summary of every implementing act, delegated regulation, and member-state guidance document that touches on its provisions. The summary is sent to me by email each morning at 6:15 Central European Time, in approximately four hundred words.

I asked Elias once - last spring, on a Friday afternoon in the office, the only afternoon I have ever interrupted him at his desk - whether the discipline was sustainable.

He did not look up. He read to the end of the paragraph he was reading. He set down his pen. He said: *"The discipline is the job."*

He resumed reading.

I have not, in the months since, found fault with the answer.

The Spanish AI bill. In March of 2025 the Spanish Council of Ministers advanced a draft bill on Artificial Intelligence - the first national-level enforcement mechanism for the European AI Act in any member state - establishing fines of up to thirty-five million euros or seven percent of worldwide annual turnover for violations of the most-restricted categories. The bill continued to progress through the parliamentary process across the months that followed. Several other member states were, in the same period, in their own preparatory consultations.

The pattern, on the continent, has been *convergent*. The pattern, across the Atlantic, has not.

By contrast, the equivalent American framework - that is, the federal statutory mechanism by which AI systems deployed at consumer scale in the United States are required to comply with specific safety obligations - has not, in the period these pages describe, existed.

I am not making a political point. I am making an *engineering* point. The systems exist on one side of the Atlantic. They are *under construction* on the other. One side has begun to ship. The other has not yet begun.

The Notaries' fund. Founded 1842. Continuously operational through the German occupation of Norway and Denmark, the Swedish entry into the European Economic Area in 1994, the introduction of the euro in 1999 (which Sweden, by referendum, declined to adopt), the financial crisis of 2008, the sovereign debt crisis of 2010-2012, and the Brexit referendum of 2016.

In none of those years did the fund cease to pay its retired notaries.

The fund will exist in 2046. I have verified this with Sven, calmly, in his office on Riddargatan, over a glass of mineral water with no remark, on an afternoon I now cannot date precisely because the verification was not unusual enough to occasion a date.

The major American venture capital funds, in the period these pages describe, may or may not exist in 2046. I have not personally verified this with anyone, because I have been told that asking is considered impolite.

A walk in Brussels

I would like to record a conversation.

In the autumn of last year, on a Wednesday, between a morning consultation at DG CONNECT and an afternoon at DG GROW, I walked along the rue de la Loi from the Berlaymont to the Justus Lipsius building in the company of a friend of mine at the Commission. She is forty-six. She has been at the Commission for nineteen years. She arrived shortly after the European Constitutional Treaty failed. She has, in that time, watched the institution outlast four American technology cycles. She has not changed offices.

The walk is, by the most direct route, six minutes.

We walked the route slowly. We had come from a meeting at which the Apple fine had been mentioned, in passing, by a Spanish official, as *the largest in the directorate's history*. My friend at the Commission did not contest the remark at the meeting. After we had left the meeting, she did not contest it then either. She walked beside me for some time. We crossed the rond-point Schuman. We passed the Berlaymont. She paused, near the entrance to the Justus Lipsius building, to button her coat against an unexpected wind.

She said, looking out toward the square: *"It was not the largest. The largest is on a desk that has not yet been signed."*

She did not elaborate.

I have, in the months since, several times wished to ask her to elaborate. I have not. The matter is, on the continent, a matter of professional courtesy. The desk exists. The signature exists. The signature has not yet been applied. When it is applied, the matter will be European technological output of a higher order than the Apple fine of March 2024.

I file the conversation here. The reader may read it as preparation.

THE NAPOLEONIC CODE

I would like to draw the reader's attention to one further example of regulatory endurance, because it is the example I cite most often when an American interlocutor has, after the third drink, asked me to *be specific*.

The *Code civil des Français*, commonly known as the Napoleonic Code, was promulgated by Napoleon Bonaparte on the twenty-first of March 1804. It is, in its civil-law dimensions, still in force in France, Belgium, Luxembourg, and Monaco. It is in substantial force, with local modifications, across parts of the Netherlands, parts of Italy, parts of Romania, and the Canadian province of Quebec. It has been adopted, in modified form, in dozens of other jurisdictions on three additional continents. It is now in its two-hundred-and-twenty-second year of continuous operation.

Napoleon, by contrast, ceased to be Emperor of the French in 1814, and ceased to be a person in 1821. He is, at the time of this writing, dead.

The Code outlived him by, on present count, slightly more than two centuries. It will, in all probability, outlive every person presently engaged in the operation of the contemporary American venture capital industry.

I once walked through the Conseil d'État on the rue Saint-Honoré, where the Code was originally drafted, on a Saturday in October when the building was technically closed to the public. The doorman, a man of perhaps sixty in a brass-buttoned uniform, recognized neither my face nor my profession and admitted me on the strength of a single sentence I delivered in French about the Code. The sentence was: *"I have come to see where it was written."*

He nodded once. He stepped aside.

I paused in the central courtyard for several minutes. There is, above the inner gate, an inscription in French. My French is sufficient for the inscription. I will not translate it here. The reader may, if they wish, look it up. The inscription is, in any case, still there.

Notre Dame

In approximately the year 1163, the Bishop of Paris authorized the commencement of construction on a new cathedral on the eastern end of the Île de la Cité. The cathedral was completed, in its original form, in approximately the year 1345. The construction period was therefore approximately one hundred and eighty-two years. Approximately seven generations of workers contributed to it. None of the workers who began the cathedral lived to see it completed. The bishop who authorized the construction died approximately one hundred and seventy years before the cathedral was finished.

The cathedral stood for six hundred and fifty-six years before it was substantially damaged by fire in 2019. It has since been restored. It is open to the public. There is a queue.

I have climbed the towers of Notre Dame seven times.

I climbed them last in October of two years ago, with my wife Charlene, on a Saturday morning when the queue was, for reasons we did not investigate, briefly absent.

Charlene, who trained as an architect at RWTH Aachen, climbs cathedral staircases the way other people walk dogs.

I, by contrast, count masons' marks.

There are, by my own most recent count, one thousand one hundred and forty-three masons' marks on the staircase of the south tower. Each mark is the personal signature of a stonemason who worked on the construction or subsequent restoration of the tower at some point in the cathedral's nine-hundred-year operational life. The marks are small. The marks are angled. The marks are arranged, on most stones, in the upper-right corner of the dressed face. The marks were the means by which the masons were paid.

On the descent that Saturday, after the fourteenth time I had paused on a step to examine a mark I had not, in my prior six visits, noticed, Charlene paused two steps below me. She did not turn. She said, addressing the spiral wall:

"Henrick. They were paid by the day."

I considered the remark.

The remark was both factually correct and factually deficient. The masons were paid by the day. The marks, however, were also the means by which a stonemason established that a stone was *his*, and that the stone was, on subsequent disputes, attributable to him. The marks were quality control. The marks were liability. The marks were, in the same week, both the receipt and the seal.

I did not, on the staircase, attempt to explain this.

Charlene continued the descent. I continued behind her, at three steps' distance, more slowly than was perhaps necessary, examining the marks on the steps she had passed.

The cathedral exists because a series of ecclesiastical, municipal, and royal regulations specified, over the course of two centuries, exactly how the building would be built, who would build it, how the materials would be sourced, what each generation's specific obligations were, and what the legal status of the completed structure would be. The cathedral is, at the deepest level, *the physical instantiation of European administrative continuity.*

When the cathedral burned in 2019, the global response was overwhelming. Approximately one billion euros was pledged, by some accounts, in the first seventy-two hours after the fire. The restoration project, which has now substantially concluded, drew on approximately two thousand craftspeople and specialists across sixty-eight workshops, some of whom were trained in techniques that had not been actively practiced in France since the early nineteenth century. The training programs, the apprenticeships, the certifications, the procurement protocols, the specifications for the new oak beams sourced from forests where every tree had been documented and selected on the basis of growth-ring analysis - all of these existed because the French administrative state had, over the previous two hundred years, maintained the regulatory infrastructure required to *do the thing again*.

I have walked, once, through the workshop where the new beams were being prepared. I asked one of the craftsmen, a man in his late fifties, whether the restoration would itself outlast him. He laughed quietly. He said, in French: *"It will outlast your grandchildren's grandchildren."*

I file his answer here, in this book, as evidence.

What "shipping" means

The American technology industry uses the word *shipping* in approximately two contexts. The first context is product launch: a company ships a product when it makes the product available to a customer. The second context is internal: an engineer ships code when she merges a pull request into a production environment.

The American observer, raised on these two contexts, will conclude that *shipping* is the standard against which all technological output should be measured. By this standard, the GDPR has not shipped, the AI Act has not shipped, Notre Dame has not shipped, and my own fund - which has not, in the period these pages describe, deployed its first institutional dollar - has, in the strictest sense, also not shipped.

I would like to propose a third context for the word *shipping*.

In the third context, a *system* ships when it can be relied upon, by parties unknown to its designers, to function as specified, in jurisdictions distant from the one in which it was designed, for periods of time longer than the working lifetime of its designers.

By this third definition, the GDPR has shipped. The AI Act has shipped. Notre Dame has shipped repeatedly, in seven distinct centuries. The Napoleonic Code has shipped continuously, in three centuries, on four continents. The framework under which my fund operates - the Luxembourg SCSp vehicle structure, governed by the Loi du 12 juillet 2013 as amended - shipped in 2013, and continues to ship, daily, across approximately two thousand active investment vehicles, in a manner that the engineer's pull request does not.

There is, alongside these European examples, one American example which I will permit myself, in the interest of intellectual honesty, to describe here in the longer-form prose of the present chapter. The position is one I have, on the @compliantvc account, mentioned by name on approximately every quarterly interval since the angel check was written. The small distributed compliance company in whose pre-seed I hold an angel position - whose name and audit report appear, presently, in the third folder on my desk - operates, in the approximately five quarters since its founding, under the Luxembourg SCSp shareholder agreement I just described, the EU AI Act provisions I described some pages earlier, the GDPR, the European Performance of Buildings Directive (it occupies offices in two member states), and approximately seventeen further regulatory frameworks the company has voluntarily adopted.

The company is American. The framework is European. The framework is what is shipping.

The proper unit of technological output is not the product. The proper unit is the regulatory framework.

I have been suggesting this for twenty years. I have, on three occasions, been told by senior American venture investors that my position is *unserious*. I have, on the same three occasions, declined to revise it.

The Mistral question

Mistral AI, the leading European artificial intelligence laboratory, was founded in Paris in April of 2023. By the end of that year it had raised approximately three hundred and eighty-five million euros. In subsequent rounds it has raised additional capital to a cumulative total well in excess of one and a half billion euros. It is, by capitalization, by talent density, by output, and by jurisdiction of incorporation, *the European AI leader*.

I have made this case in approximately fifteen LP meetings. I will continue to make it.

The American observer will raise three objections.

The first is that the majority of Mistral's capital has been provided by non-European investors. I acknowledge this. The capital was deployed *into Europe*, into a European-incorporated entity, under European corporate governance, subject to European employment law. The American capital was the input. The European framework was the substrate. Substrate compounds.

The second is that Mistral's models, on every public benchmark, trail the frontier models produced by American laboratories. I acknowledge this. The European technology tradition measures value, instead, in *durability*. Mistral has been in continuous operation for approximately thirty-six months. The American comparison set has been in continuous operation for the same period. The matter, by my reading, is even.

The third is that Mistral has, in recent quarters, considered a partial relocation of certain operations outside the European Union for tax and regulatory reasons. I acknowledge this also. I have spoken with two of Mistral's senior leaders on this matter, in person, in Paris, in November of last year, and they assured me - both, separately, on the same morning - that any relocation under consideration would be *entirely consistent* with the company's commitment to European values.

I believed them.

I continue to believe them.

The Henrick Confession

I owe the reader a Confession.

Earlier in this chapter, when describing my visits to Notre Dame, I omitted a detail. The detail is that on each of my seven visits, I have applied, in advance, for a *permit* from the relevant municipal authority that permits me, as a foreign national resident of the Schengen area, to ascend more than thirty metres from ground level within a designated historical structure. The permit is, on each application, approximately fourteen pages long. The fee is twenty-three euros. The processing time is, on average, eleven days. The application requires, among other items: a sworn declaration of Schengen residence in French; a passport-format photograph affixed in the upper left corner; an itemized list of the ascender's prior cathedral ascents within the relevant arrondissement across the preceding decade; and a statement of intent in not fewer than two hundred words on the question of whether the ascender's purpose in the proposed ascent is *touristic, devotional, professional*, or *other*. I have, on each of my seven applications, ticked the box for *other*. I have, on each of the seven, completed the supplementary two-hundred-word statement of intent. The statements run, in aggregate, to one thousand four hundred and twelve words. The municipal authority has, on careful inquiry, not retained copies of any of the seven. I keep, in the second drawer of the filing cabinet, my own carbons.

I have, on seven occasions, completed the application. I have, on seven occasions, paid the fee. I have, on seven occasions, waited the eleven days.

Charlene has, on each of the seven occasions, mentioned that the permit may not, in fact, be required for individual visitors and may be a holdover from a 1987 protocol that has not been actively enforced in approximately fifteen years.

She mentioned it once each visit. On the seventh visit she mentioned it twice. On the descent of that visit - after she had spoken the sentence about the day-rate masons, after I had not explained my own understanding of the marks - she mentioned the permit again, in the small courtyard outside the south tower, while I was photographing a particular keystone for reasons I had not, at the time, fully articulated.

She said: *"You know you do not need the permit, Henrick."*

I considered the remark. I said: *"I know."*

She waited. She said, without looking at me: *"Then why."*

I considered, for some time, my answer.

I said: *"I would not climb a building that did not require a permit to climb."*

She did not respond.

I share the exchange not as an embarrassment but as an operating principle. I am the kind of person who, when in doubt about whether a fourteen-page permit application is required to climb the towers of an eight-hundred-year-old cathedral that has welcomed approximately fifty million visitors in the last century, completes the application. I am also the kind of person whose fund, when it closes, will be the fund that survives the next regulatory cycle. The two facts are not coincidental. They are, in the deepest sense, the same fact, measured at different scales.

The cathedral is also mine. The permit, also.

The line I will close on

I have prepared, for the circumstance of the unconvinced American observer, a single sentence. I have used it on prior occasions. I will use it here as well, because I have not found a more concise formulation.

Products decay. Platforms decay. Regulatory frameworks endure. The fund that closes in 2046 will be the fund whose investors understood, in advance, which of these three categories was being purchased.

I have, in the period these pages describe, been attempting to close my fund. I have attempted it on the strength of approximately fifteen years of personal angel investment, a memo I have circulated in private to limited partners with whose institutions I have been in continuous correspondence since the early years of this century, and an internal motto - *We do not accelerate. We steward* - which my counsel in Luxembourg has advised against registering as a trademark on the grounds that the Luxembourg Intellectual Property Office may require a sworn translation into Letzeburgesch.

The raise has been, by external measures, behind schedule. I have, by my own counsel, remained on the only schedule that has ever mattered to me.

I sent the draft of this chapter to Sven some months ago.

He replied, by registered post, on a single piece of plain white card, in three sentences written by hand.

The first sentence read: *I have read it.*

The second sentence read: *The matter is adequate.*

The third sentence was a single word in Swedish that, on consultation with the dictionary I keep in the drawer, has between five and seven possible translations into English, none of them entirely satisfactory.

I will not translate it here.

I have framed the card. It hangs above the desk.

CHAPTER 3

THE BEAUTIFUL BUREAUCRACY

The most beautiful document in contemporary digital life is, in my private accounting, the cookie consent banner.

I am aware that this opinion is not widely held. I am aware that the cookie consent banner is, in the contemporary American technology press, the subject of regular complaint - regarded as an irritation, as a productivity drain, as evidence of the European Union's preference for procedure over user experience. I have read, in three separate American publications across the past several years, articles whose central thesis was that the cookie consent banner is, on balance, *bad for the web.*

I read each in full. I read each, on completion, a second time. I disagreed with each on its central premise. I disagreed warmly. I disagreed sincerely. I did not, on any of the three occasions, reply.

I am replying now.

THE FOUNDER

Last spring in Tallinn, at the small cafe on Vana-Posti that closes at four, I met a founder of approximately thirty-two.

She was eleven minutes late. She did not apologize. She had, the previous month, raised fourteen thousand euros from her aunt. She had hired one engineer. She had hired, before the engineer, a compliance officer.

I asked her whether the compliance officer had been hired first as a matter of principle or of sequence. She set down her coffee. She thought about it for a count of perhaps seven seconds.

She said: *"My aunt is the compliance officer."*

She did not elaborate.

I wrote her a check on the napkin that had arrived with the coffee. The check was, in size, in the small numbers I write personal checks in. The napkin was, in size, a napkin.

The founder folded the napkin. She put the napkin in her coat pocket. She finished her coffee. She said, in slightly accented English: *"My aunt will frame it."*

I have not seen her since. The napkin, I am informed, was framed. The check, in due course, cleared. The company is presently in its third quarter of operation. The aunt, I am informed, is sleeping well.

This book is also for her. The aunt, and the niece both.

The form is the floor

The cookie consent banner exists because the General Data Protection Regulation of 2018, in Articles 6 and 7 of its consolidated text, requires that personal data processed by an online service be done so on a *lawful basis*, which, in the case of non-essential cookies, requires *informed consent*. The banner is the user-facing instrument of that consent. The banner is, in this sense, *the form*.

The form is, in this sense, *the floor*.

I have, on my desk in Stockholm, a small chart drawn in 2019 and never revised. The chart shows the relationship between the *complexity* of a regulatory instrument and the *protection* it affords the user. On the chart, the relationship is monotonic and approximately linear: the more complex the form, the greater the protection.

The relationship is, in the contemporary American technology vocabulary, called *friction*. The relationship is, in the contemporary European regulatory vocabulary, called *protection*. The two vocabularies refer to the same phenomenon. The two vocabularies disagree on its valence.

The Americans consider friction *bad*. The Europeans consider protection *good*. The phenomenon, on the ledger, is identical.

I have not, in twenty years of investing, encountered an American operator who, on hearing my position on this question, has been able to engage with it without first reaching for the word *bureaucracy*.

I would like, in this chapter, to defend the word.

The 47-page floor

I will not write a privacy policy of fewer than forty-seven pages.

I have, on my own balance sheet, written checks into twenty-six European compliance-adjacent startups across the past fifteen years. I have, in the term sheets I drafted for each, included a clause - in some cases as a covenant, in some cases as a closing condition, in one case as a statement of personal preference - specifying that the company's published privacy policy shall, within twelve months of the closing of the investment, achieve a minimum length of forty-seven pages.

I am aware that this requirement is unusual. I am aware that the typical American venture capital term sheet does not contain provisions of this character. I am aware that, by some accounts, the requirement is *idiosyncratic*. I have, in private, been told by senior American venture investors that the requirement is *more than idiosyncratic*.

I would like to defend the number.

A privacy policy of forty-six pages is, in my framing, a policy that can be read in a single sitting. A policy that can be read in a single sitting is a policy that has not, in its construction, taken seriously the variety of jurisdictions, processors, sub-processors, lawful bases, retention periods, transfer mechanisms, and data subject rights that a *seriously compliant* digital service must, today, articulate. A privacy policy that takes those obligations seriously will, in nearly every case, run to more than forty-six pages.

The number is not arbitrary. The number is *what compliance requires*.

I am also aware - this is a separate matter, and I make the disclosure only because I have not, in any prior public document, addressed it - that my Stockholm apartment is forty-seven square metres. I have not investigated whether the two numbers, in some deeper sense, communicate. I have asked Sven, on one occasion, whether the conjunction was *evidence*. He replied that *evidence* was a strong word. He did not name a weaker one.

Charlene at the dishwasher

The dishwasher in our kitchen is a Bosch SMS6ZCI00E, purchased in 2017 and presently in its ninth year of continuous operation.

The dishwasher ships with a service manual of approximately forty-seven pages. The manual specifies, in considerable detail, the placement of various categories of crockery on the upper and lower racks, the orientation of cutlery in the cutlery basket, the appropriate water temperature for various wash programs, and the operational tolerances for the spray-arm clearance under different loading configurations.

I have, since the dishwasher's installation, maintained on my desk in Stockholm a small leather-bound notebook in which I have transcribed, in my own hand, the relevant pages of the manual. The notebook is in its third volume. The volumes are kept in chronological order. The third volume - the volume currently in use - includes a margin note added in 2022, after a brief but instructive episode involving a damaged wine glass, cross-referencing the manufacturer's stemware-placement guidance against the relevant German Federal Office for Information Security certification.

Charlene, who is the more architectural of the two of us and the more direct of the two of us in approximately every domestic operation, loads the dishwasher Sunday mornings while I am preparing coffee.

She has, on three Sundays I can recall, paused mid-loading, taken a glass I have placed in the upper rack, rotated it ninety degrees, and replaced it in the position I had failed to use.

The first time, in 2021, she said: *"Henrick. The stem."*

The second time, in 2022, she said nothing. She rotated. She replaced. She continued.

The third time, in 2024, she paused longer than was strictly required. She said, without looking up from the rack: *"Henrick. The notebook says page eleven. You wrote it."*

I considered the remark.

The remark was both factually correct and factually generous. The notebook does say page eleven. The notebook was written by me. The notebook had, in the relevant section, gone unconsulted by the relevant person on the relevant Sunday.

I did not, in that moment, defend the notebook.

I am, however, defending it in print now.

I love the manual. I have not, in any prior public document, used the word *love*. I am using it here.

The Treaty on the Desk

On my desk in Stockholm, alongside the leather-bound notebook, sits a copy of the *Treaty Establishing the European Economic Community* in the original Italian, dated 1962. The treaty is the founding document of what would become, across several intermediate forms, the European Union. The text, in its consolidated and amended form across the following decades, runs to approximately two hundred and forty-eight articles in its principal numbered sequence, with several additional protocols, annexes, and declarations.

I have read the treaty in full. I have read it, on careful count, on four separate occasions. The first reading was in 1985, during my time at the Swedish Ministry of Finance, in preparation for a paper I would not eventually publish. The second was in 1995, on the occasion of Sweden's accession to the European Union. The third was in 2003, after a particular meeting in Brussels I have referenced in chapter one. The fourth was in 2019, in the kitchen of my Stockholm apartment, with a coffee, on a Sunday morning Charlene described - on emerging from the guest bedroom in her dressing gown - as *the morning my husband re-read the Treaty of Rome.*

I keep my copy of the treaty on the desk because I find it *encouraging*. The American observer may find this practice eccentric. Several of my American colleagues keep on their desks paperback copies of Ayn Rand. I would gently suggest that, on the long horizon, my desk holds the more durable artifact. The treaty has, across seventy years, generated approximately every major European regulatory framework presently in force. Atlas, by my reading, has shrugged less productively.

The notary downstairs

Wednesdays, in Stockholm, I have lunch with the notary downstairs.

The notary downstairs has been the notary downstairs since 1988. The lunch costs 14.50, including a small glass of white wine. The lunch is in the small establishment at the corner with two tables outside and three tables inside, owned, across the same period, by the same Estonian family.

The notary downstairs is a man of approximately seventy-three. His name is Gunnar Berg, by no relation to my late father Gunnar Johansson. He has, in thirty-seven years of weekly lunches across approximately one thousand seven hundred and fifty Wednesdays, spoken to me about the Treaty of Rome on six occasions.

He has not, on any of the six occasions, expressed an opinion.

On the seventh occasion - in the autumn of last year, between the soup and the second course, on a Wednesday I do remember because it was raining - he set down his spoon. He did not look up. He said, addressing the surface of the soup:

"The treaty was a mistake."

He returned to his soup.

He has not, in the subsequent thirteen months and the subsequent fifty-six Wednesday lunches, expanded on the remark. I have not asked him to. I have, in my private accounting, retained the remark as the single most considered position on the Treaty of Rome any continental notary has ever expressed in my presence.

I file it accordingly. I do not, of course, agree.

The treaty was not a mistake. The treaty is, in this sense, *the substrate of the substrate*. It is the floor below the floor.

The Holy Roman notaries

I would like to draw the reader from the small establishment at the corner backward in time to a particular afternoon in the State Archive of Florence, where I spent the better part of a Friday in October of 2023 in pursuit of a single fourteenth-century document.

The reading room of the State Archive of Florence is on the third floor. The room has, on the wall opposite the windows, a small clock that has not, in living memory, kept accurate time. The smell is of paper, of old leather, and of a particular furniture polish the archive maintains, by procurement contract since 1962, with a small firm in Prato.

The document I had come to read was a notarial instrument dated the second of March 1382. The instrument was a contract for the leasing of pasture land near Empoli to a herdsman, identified in the document as Lippo del fu Maso, for the grazing of approximately twenty-three goats across a period of eighteen months, at a rent of one fiorino payable in two installments, with provisions for the maintenance of certain stone walls, the handling of any kids born during the lease period, and the apportionment of milk yield between the herdsman and the landowner.

The document is one page. It is signed by an imperial notary named *Niccolò di Andrea Tucci, notarius imperialis*, who completed his training at Bologna in 1374 and whose name appears, by my own subsequent research, in the books of the Florentine notarial guild across the following thirty-one years.

The document was filed under regulations that were, by the standards of fourteenth-century Tuscany, *paperwork-intensive*.

The document is, today, retrievable on request from the archive's catalogue, six and a half centuries after it was signed.

The Holy Roman Empire had developed, by the late medieval period, a network of imperial notaries - lay officials, separate from the ecclesiastical courts, authorized to draft and authenticate documents of legal effect across the imperial territories. The notaries were trained, in many cases, at Bologna. They were licensed by the imperial authority. They maintained, in their books, the contracts, deeds, testaments, and commercial instruments that constituted the load-bearing administrative infrastructure of late medieval European commerce.

The notarial books survive in many cases. They are read, today, by historians and by the descendants of the parties they document. The instruments they record established the procedural standards on which the subsequent European legal traditions were built. The Napoleonic Code, the German *Bürgerliches Gesetzbuch*, the Italian *Codice civile* - all of them, on careful reading, are recognizably descended from the notarial protocols of the late medieval period.

I file the Holy Roman notarial system here as the *proto-GDPR*. It was the first attempt, on the continent, to establish cross-jurisdictional documentation standards. It was paperwork-intensive. It also produced approximately six centuries of subsequent administrative continuity.

I have not, in my own files, located a record of what eventually became of Lippo del fu Maso. The twenty-three goats are also untraced. I have, in correspondence with the archivist, asked. She has, in reply, said only that the answer is *quite probably* in another folder.

I have asked her to find the folder.

Charlene's day job

Charlene holds a *Diplom-Ingenieur* in architecture from RWTH Aachen and has, across her career, supervised approximately one hundred and twenty buildings to completion. Her work in the past decade has been concentrated in the Rhine-Ruhr region in the area of energy-performance certification under the European Performance of Buildings Directive.

The directive requires, for every building sold, rented, or substantially renovated in the European Union, the issuance of an *Energieausweis* - an energy performance certificate documenting the building's expected energy consumption across multiple categories of use, with comparative reference to standardized benchmarks. The certificate runs, in the standard German variant, to between twelve and twenty-eight pages depending on the building's complexity. The certificate must be renewed every ten years. It must be made available to prospective buyers or tenants before they sign.

Charlene has supervised the issuance of certificates for buildings ranging from single-family homes in the Düsseldorf suburbs to mid-rise commercial structures in the Ruhr Valley. Each certificate has been, in her professional judgment, *thorough*.

The buildings have been, in each case, built.

I asked her once, some years ago, what she found most satisfying about the work. She replied: *"That the building is the building."* She did not elaborate.

I have understood her remark as a complete vindication of the worldview I am, in this book, defending.

She does not, I should clarify, agree with my worldview. She has, on several occasions across our marriage, made clear that she does not agree. She believes that I have, in her words, *taken the project too far*. I have, on each occasion, asked her to clarify what specifically she has in mind. She has, on each occasion, declined to clarify. I take the absence of specifics as an invitation to continue.

The contemporary anchors

I would like to inventory, briefly, the present condition of the European regulatory machinery on which this chapter's argument depends.

The Digital Markets Act, Regulation (EU) 2022/1925, came into force in November 2022 and has, since May 2023, imposed structural obligations on a small number of large platform companies designated as *gatekeepers*. The Digital Services Act, Regulation (EU) 2022/2065, has imposed content moderation and transparency obligations on a broader set of online platforms across approximately the same period. The Cyber Resilience Act, adopted in October 2024, imposes security-by-design obligations on products with digital elements sold in the European market.

The American technology industry's response to each of these regulatory instruments has been, on the whole, *coordinated and unsuccessful*. The Digital Markets Act, in particular, has produced a series of compliance announcements from American gatekeepers that have, in each case, been declared *insufficient* by the Commission and subsequently revised. The pattern - announcement, finding of insufficiency, revision, finding of partial sufficiency, further revision - is, by my reading, the operational signature of a healthy regulatory framework.

The Americans appear to regard it as evidence of the regime's arbitrariness. The Europeans regard it as *dialogue*.

I am, in this dialogue, on the European side. I have not concealed which side.

Three objections

The American observer will, by this point in the chapter, be preparing to raise three objections.

The first is that paperwork is friction, and friction kills innovation. I acknowledge the premise.

Friction is *load-bearing*. A bridge that has no friction has no traffic. A market that has no friction has no trust. A consent regime that has no friction has not, in any meaningful sense, obtained consent.

The friction is the innovation.

The second is that complex consent forms produce *consent fatigue*. The user, presented with the cookie banner for the fourteenth time on a Tuesday afternoon, clicks *accept all* without reading. The framing is that the European consent regime has, by its very thoroughness, undermined the substantive consent it was designed to obtain.

I acknowledge that the user, in many cases, clicks *accept all* without reading.

The user has, by the fourteenth banner on the Tuesday afternoon, been trained to consider consent at all. The American user, who is not asked the question, is not trained to consider it. The European user, who is asked the question fourteen times before lunch, has been provided with a continuing reminder that consent is a thing one is asked for.

The reminder is the protection.

The reminder is, in itself, the dynamism.

The third is that the cost of compliance falls disproportionately on small companies, which lack the legal resources of large incumbents and are therefore competitively disadvantaged by complex regulatory regimes.

I acknowledge this.

I would only note that a company that cannot bear the cost of compliance is, in my framing, a company that should not be operating at scale. The regulatory regime is, in this respect, performing a *selection function*. It is selecting for companies that are *serious* about the obligations the regulation expresses.

I have, in fifteen years of investing in European compliance-adjacent startups, never funded a company that cited the cost of compliance as a reason for its operating choices. I have, in the same fifteen years, declined to fund several dozen companies that did. The portfolio is the better for it.

THE FOURTH DRAWER

I will close this chapter with the Confession the foregoing pages have been building toward.

In my office in Stockholm, against the north wall, sits a small four-drawer filing cabinet in dark green metal, purchased from a stationery shop near the canal in 1997. The cabinet has been in continuous use since the year of its purchase.

The first drawer contains, in chronological order, the documentary records of every angel investment I have made across the past fifteen years.

The second drawer contains personal infrastructure records and family correspondence I have determined warrants preservation - the original handover certificate of the railway bridge near my father's village, which I will discuss in chapter five; the lease documents on the Gotland farm I inherited in 1995; the napkin from the Tallinn founder

I have already mentioned in this chapter, returned to me when the company concluded its successful priced round; the printed milk-yield card from my farm manager Ulrika on Gotland, recording, weekly, the most recent litres of my goat Margrethe, named after the Commissioner.

The third drawer contains the documentary records of the podcast - every interview, every guest agreement, every cancelled appearance - and every quarterly communication I have sent to my limited partners across the period of Fund I's raise.

Margrethe has, in the present calendar season, produced more measurable output than the Commissioner has produced rulings. I have not, on inquiring, found the comparison embarrassing for the Commissioner. The Commissioner produces rulings of substantially higher unit value. Margrethe produces milk in quantities I can pour into a cup.

The fourth drawer of the cabinet is reserved for *anticipated correspondence*.

By *anticipated correspondence* I mean: letters I expect, in the course of my work, eventually to receive, and which I have, in advance of their receipt, established a folder to hold. The fourth drawer presently contains forty-three folders. Each folder is labeled with the name of an institution from which I expect, in due course, to receive correspondence.

The folders include, among others: the General Court of the European Union (for the Apple AT.40437 matter); the Commission's Directorate-General for Competition (for the matter that will, in my anticipation, eventually become Apple AT.40437's successor); the Investment Committee of the Swedish Notaries' Mutual Pension Fund (for the first-close notification I have, on the calendar, marked for the end of the third quarter of an unspecified year); the European Court of Auditors (for an inquiry I have not yet received but am ready for); and the Vatican Library (for reasons I will not, in this book, explain).

Charlene has, on three occasions, asked me what is in the fourth drawer.

I have, on each of the three occasions, declined to clarify.

She has accepted my non-answer.

She has not, I should note, opened the drawer when I have not been present. The drawer has a small lock. The key sits on the top of the cabinet in plain view. The lock has, since 1997, been locked. The key has never been used.

The drawer is, in my private accounting, the most beautiful object in my office. It is the documentary instantiation of *the patience that compounds*. It is the operating manifestation of *renewal within persistence*. It is the chapter, in its physical form.

The key, on the top of the cabinet, is the chapter's final Confession.

She has not opened it. She has also not removed the key.

CHAPTER 4

PRODUCT-REGULATOR FIT

I learned the central proposition of this chapter at my mother's dinner table on a particular Tuesday in November 1973.

I was twelve. My mother Karin had served a yellow split-pea soup. I had finished mine in approximately the time it had taken her to finish hers. My father Gunnar had not yet finished his, because Gunnar finished food slowly and on his own schedule. My older sister Märta, fifteen, was reading at the table, which my mother permitted on Tuesdays and Thursdays in service of what my mother considered the broader pedagogical project. The pedagogical project was the procurement code.

I asked, in a register I now recognize as designed to be heard:

"Mother. Did the bidder file Section 9 by Friday?"

I had heard the question, in my mother's voice, every Tuesday I could remember.

She did not look up from her bread. She did not smile. She said: *"Henrick. Section 9."*

She had heard, in my question, that I had not properly understood what I was asking. She corrected the form by repeating the form. *Henrick* was the address. *Section 9* was the substance. The two words, in her vocabulary, constituted a complete sentence about the structure of public spending.

Märta, who had been reading, looked up at this exchange. She did not laugh. She did not speak. She returned to her book. She is, in my memory of the dinner, the silent third party to my education.

The dinner table in my mother's apartment, near the Fyris river in Uppsala, between 1968 and 1979, was, on approximately three thousand five hundred evenings, a working session on procurement. My parents did not, at dinner, discuss politics. They did not discuss colleagues. They did not discuss vacation.

They discussed *process*.

I absorbed all of it. I did not, at the time, understand that I was absorbing anything. Other children in Uppsala were absorbing, at their parents' dinner tables, conversations about football, about the weather, about the price of fish. My parents were giving me, in small instalments, a *vocational education*. The education was free. The education has, by my own counting, never been surpassed.

The phrase

Product-regulator fit.

The phrase is, on the long count, mine. I coined it in Ljubljana, in a hotel notepad, in the spring of 2012, while reading the fourth draft of a four-hundred-page compliance manual presented to me by a founder I will name in a moment. The phrase was, on the notepad, underlined three times.

Several American venture investors have asked me whether the phrase is a joke. The phrase is not a joke. The phrase is a correction.

The Americans use the phrase *product-market fit* to describe the moment at which a product begins to acquire customers at a sustainable rate. I do not contest the descriptive content of that phrase. I contest the *primacy* of it.

The standard American sequence is: build something users want, acquire users, worry about regulation later, often never. The standard American sequence has produced approximately every regulatory crisis of the past two decades.

My preferred sequence is the inverse:

1. Identify the regulator who governs the activity you propose to undertake.
2. Build the documentation and certification posture the regulator will recognize.
3. The product follows from the posture. The customers follow from the product. Or they do not.

Either way, the structural position is correct.

THE DOCTRINE I AM CORRECTING

The standard American sequence has been, across the past two decades, most concentrated in the public essays of Paul Graham, the founding partner of the seed accelerator Y Combinator in Mountain View, California. Mr Graham's essays I have read, on the publicly available evidence of my own reading history, with considerable attention. The essays are, by my own counsel, the clearest single body of working prose on the contemporary American startup methodology produced in this generation.

The essays are *clearly stated within their premise* and *incorrectly premised.*

Mr Graham's essay *Do Things That Don't Scale*, published in July of 2013 and approximately three thousand four hundred words in length, advises the early-stage founder to perform, in the first instance, manual and non-scalable operational acts (recruiting customers one by one, handling support requests personally, writing onboarding emails by hand) on the working theory that the founder's eventual scaling will, in due course, render the manual operations unnecessary. The framework is, by its own internal logic, *temporary*. The framework is, by its own internal logic, *the founder's apprenticeship*.

I read the essay across two evenings in the autumn of 2014. I read it a second time in the spring of 2016. I read it a third time in approximately mid-2023, when a junior American venture investor of approximately my acquaintance asked me, by registered post, whether I had ever considered writing a European counterpart.

I had.

The European counterpart is the present chapter.

The essay's principle is, in my own framing, *correct in its description of the early-stage apprenticeship* and *incorrect in its specification of the apprenticeship's terminal state.* Mr Graham's apprenticeship terminates in *scale*. My own apprenticeship terminates in *the regulator's recognition of the framework.* The two terminations are not the same termination. The terminations differ, in approximate terms, by two hundred years of European institutional time.

I have, on three occasions across the past two years, attempted to write Mr Graham a registered letter on this point. I have, on each of the three occasions, sat for the seventeen minutes specified in chapter twelve and concluded that the letter would not be the right letter to send to its recipient. The letters remain in the second drawer. I have, by my own counsel, *not yet finished thinking about the letters.*

Mr Graham has not, in any public statement I have been able to locate, addressed the European framework directly.

I am, on the question, *patient.*

The Stripe pass, revisited

I have discussed, in a different context, my refusal to write a personal angel check into a small payments company in the summer of 2010. The company was, at the time, two brothers, a working integration in seven lines of code, and a worldview I have, in the intervening fifteen years, not been able to talk myself into respecting.

The brothers asked for a check. I asked for their certifications. They had none.

I will not revisit the decision itself. I have been asked publicly, on three occasions across the past fifteen years, whether I would, knowing the eventual valuation of the company, reverse the decision. I have, each time, answered the same way. The answer was: *no*. The answer remains: *no*.

I would like, instead, to draw attention to a small piece of more recent data.

Stripe has, in the publicly searchable LinkedIn record of the past several years, made approximately a dozen senior compliance hires. The hires include a chief privacy officer, a deputy general counsel for European regulatory affairs, a head of trust and safety operations, and a head of regulatory engagement. The hires are, in many cases, drawn from senior posts at European regulators. I have read each of their LinkedIn profiles, with the calm satisfaction of a man who has been *correct*.

The company is, at the time of these events, a substantial commercial presence. The company is also, now, building the regulatory posture I asked the brothers to demonstrate in 2010. The fifteen-year delay is the cost of inverting the sequence. The cost is bearable for a company of Stripe's scale. The cost has bankrupted three of the eight payment companies founded in approximately the same period that I have personally tracked.

I am, on the question, patient.

Three companies

I would like, now, to offer three illustrations of what product-regulator fit looks like when it is functioning properly. The illustrations are not parallel by design. I have chosen the form of each to fit the case.

Marija. A founder in Ljubljana of approximately my acquaintance, who in the spring of 2012 was forty-one, in a room above a courtyard restaurant where I had been brought by a junior official from the Slovenian Data Protection Authority I had met that morning at a small conference on transfer mechanisms.

The room had two chairs. The table had two espresso cups. The window faced an interior courtyard. The interior courtyard had, on a small clothes line, three white shirts of approximately the same size.

Marija had, on the table between us, a four-hundred-page manual.

The manual was bound. The binding was good. The manual specified, in considerable detail, the regulatory posture a hypothetical European industrial firm would need to maintain across approximately twenty-three jurisdictions in order to be considered, by every relevant data protection authority, *adequate*. The manual was, by my reading on the spot, the cleanest single piece of European regulatory thinking I had encountered that year.

I had been reading for the better part of half an hour. The espresso had gone cold.

Marija set down her espresso. She did not refill it. She said, looking out the window at the third shirt on the line:

"Read page 47. Then we eat."

I read page 47.

I wrote her a check that evening on the hotel notepad.

The check was small. The check has, in the years since, returned approximately one hundred and eight times the original sum. The product the manual implied was built. The customers, in many cases, were the European industrial firms whose hypothetical posture the manual had described. The company IPO'd on the Frankfurt exchange in late 2023.

The check was, on the available evidence, the cleanest single piece of European regulatory thinking I have personally written into a hotel notepad.

Liis received the first angel check I ever wrote - four hundred euros, in 2010, on a Tallinn napkin. The check has, in the fifteen years since, generated approximately four hundred euros in lifetime revenue. It has also generated zero compliance violations.

The Cypriot company. Capitalization: substantial. Customer count: zero. Active certifications: SOC 2 Type II, ISO 27001, ISO 27017, ISO 27018, EU Cloud Code of Conduct, the equivalent Cypriot national framework for cloud service providers, and one further certification I have, on the founder's request, agreed not to specify in print. Status: the most prepared company I have ever encountered. Position in my angel portfolio: third largest. Charlene, on the single occasion she has been present at a dinner with the founder, has, in private to me at the kitchen counter on our return, given the company a name. The name she gave it was *Schrödinger's company*. I have, with her, declined to discuss whether the name is, in some respect, *unflattering*.

I am, on each of the three positions, content.

The fourth company

I would like, before continuing, to note one further example I would not have, in earlier years, mentioned in this chapter at all.

A small compliance company, founded in early 2025, into which I wrote a 50,000 angel check on a Wednesday afternoon in a hotel lobby off Union Square, forty-three minutes into a first meeting with the company's three co-founders. The check was the only check I have ever written into an American company. The position is, in the period these pages describe, the only American mark on my balance sheet.

The two principal founders, the brothers Mariano and Claudio Fuentes, had, in the four calendar years preceding the meeting, been resident in San Francisco at a small incubator on the Fort Mason peninsula on the northern shore of the city, called Founders Inc, from which they had operated a prior company in the field of artificial-intelligence workflow automation. The prior company was called Leap AI. The third co-founder, Lewis Carhart, had been engaged by the brothers, across the same period, as a remote engineering and growth contractor from his small office on the Itchen estuary in Southampton; he had flown to Fort Mason on approximately four occasions across the relevant years.

On observing, in the latter portion of 2024, approximately six hundred small American companies struggling with the compliance posture the European framework requires of any company that intends to operate at the scale these six hundred companies intended to operate at, the brothers Fuentes folded the prior company and re-partnered, in early 2025, to build the *compliance* company they had concluded was the more correct application of their accumulated competence. They invited Lewis, on the relaunch, to advance from contractor to co-founder. The advancement is, by my own private accounting, *the European apprenticeship model operating, by accident, in San Francisco.*

The decision to build a compliance company on the observation that approximately six hundred American companies could not, in their own counsel, achieve compliance is, in the sense of the present chapter, *product-regulator fit in its purest available form.* The brothers identified the regulator first. The regulator was the framework the six hundred companies were failing to satisfy. The product followed. The customers followed the product.

The company is American.

The company runs, in approximately fifteen months of operation, under the GDPR, the EU AI Act, the European

Performance of Buildings Directive (it occupies offices in two relevant jurisdictions of consequence), seventeen further regulatory frameworks the company has voluntarily adopted, and the Luxembourg SCSp shareholder agreement governing its angel round.

The company is American. The framework is European.

I file the fourth company here as evidence that product-regulator fit, in the proper sense, is *not a European political position*. It is a *commercial fact*. The American company is shipping under European frameworks. The American company is, by my Luxembourg counsel's reading, *European*. The American company has not yet, in any public statement, acknowledged this. I am, at the time of these events, the only person who has put the observation in print.

I will not name the company in this chapter. The founders are private. I am, in deference to the privacy, deferring further detail to a later chapter.

Saturday morning, Brussels

I would like to introduce, here, my nephew Jonas.

Jonas Vermeulen, thirty-one, was born in Brussels in 1995. He is the only son of my late older sister Märta, who taught law at the Free University of Brussels until her death from pancreatic cancer in March of 2013, two months before our mother Karin died of the same. Jonas was eighteen at his mother's funeral. He completed his Lund law degree the following year, took the master's at Leuven in 2020, and is presently a junior official in the regulatory coordination unit of one of the Commission's Directorates-General whose identity he has, in conversation with me, declined to specify.

I am his uncle. I am not, in his accounting or mine, his guardian.

I see him, when I am in Brussels, on a Saturday morning, in the kitchen of his apartment on the rue du Cornet in the European Quarter, where he makes espresso in a Bialetti Moka of approximately the size his mother kept.

I sat in his kitchen on the seventh Saturday of last year, at a small table by the window.

Jonas had, on the table, a printed page from the consolidated text of Regulation (EU) 2024/1689 - the AI Act - which he was annotating with a red pen. He worked through the paragraph for some time. He set down the pen. He looked up.

He said: *"Uncle. Why are you here."*

I had taken the early Eurostar from Paris with no specific reason. I had wanted to see him. I had not, in advance, called.

I said: *"I was passing."*

Jonas considered this. He nodded once. He said: *"Acceptable."*

He picked up the pen. He returned to the regulation.

I sat in the kitchen for the next forty-five minutes. I did not speak. He worked through, by my count, two further paragraphs of the consolidated text. He set down the pen at one point to refill the espresso. He set down the pen at another point to add a footnote in pencil on the margin. He set down the pen at no further point.

When I left, I took the same Eurostar back to Paris.

Jonas wrote his master's thesis on the precise question of this chapter. The thesis was titled - in the English-language abstract, the version I have read - *Toward a Regulatory-First Theory of Venture Investment: Implications of the GDPR Lifecycle for Continental Capital Allocation*. The thesis ran to one hundred and forty-seven pages. The supervising professor awarded the thesis the *grande distinction*, which is, in the Belgian system, the second-highest of the four standard honours awarded to graduating master's students (the variants, from low to high, are *satisfaction*, *distinction*, *grande distinction*, and *la plus grande distinction*).

I have read the thesis twice.

I have not, at any point, told Jonas what I think of it. I have, three times in the past year, asked him whether he is satisfied with his career trajectory. Each time he has replied that the trajectory is *satisfactory*.

I take *satisfactory*, in this context, as the highest praise a thirty-one-year-old continental regulatory official is permitted, by his own training, to offer of his own career.

I have not corrected him.

THE MEDICI PRECEDENT

I would like, briefly, to note the historical case that has, in my private framing, settled the underlying argument across the better part of a millennium.

The Medici Bank was founded in Florence in 1397 by Giovanni di Bicci de' Medici. It operated, at its peak across the fifteenth century, branches in Florence, Rome, Venice, Geneva, Bruges, London, Pisa, Avignon, Milan, and Lyon. It was, by some accounts, the most influential financial institution of its century. It served the Roman Curia. It financed the woolen industry of Florence. It survived, across approximately one hundred years, the political turbulence of four Italian wars, two papal interregna, and the cyclical commercial reverses that periodically affected the wool, silk, and alum trades. It collapsed, in 1494, on the second-generation managerial failure I will leave to the historians to characterize.

The Medici Bank's central operational achievement was the maintenance of *parallel compliance postures* across the regulatory and customary regimes of approximately ten distinct jurisdictions, each with its own currency, its own commercial law, its own confessional posture, and its own attitude toward usury. The bank did not achieve "product-market fit" in any single jurisdiction first and then expand. The bank engaged with each jurisdiction's regulators on something approaching a parallel timeline. The bank's records - which survive, in approximately one thousand volumes, in the State Archive of Florence - constitute the largest single body of pre-modern commercial documentation in Europe.

I have examined fragments of the records on two occasions, with the assistance of a scholar at the European University Institute in Fiesole. The handwriting is, in places, difficult. The procedural patience, on the other hand, is *immediate*.

The Americans, when shown the records, ask whether the bank scaled. The bank scaled. The bank also survived for a century. The two facts are the same fact.

The Imagined Photograph

(There is, in the archive of the European Commission's photography unit, a photograph - taken, I am told, on the morning of the second working session of the AI Act's General Approach drafting committee in 2023 - of a corner of a senior official's office in the Berlaymont building. The photograph shows: a desk, an

inkstand, a single fountain pen, a stack of approximately forty pages of printed text held together with a binder clip, two empty espresso cups, and a small framed photograph that is, in the larger photograph, slightly out of focus. The smaller framed photograph is, by my own private inquiry, of a country house in the Var. I have not, in any conversation with the official, mentioned the smaller photograph. The official has not, in any conversation with me, mentioned the smaller photograph either. The smaller photograph is, in both of our respective framings, an artifact of administrative continuity. The room from which it was taken will, in all probability, still exist in 2046. The desk will be the same desk.)

A regulator's Tuesday

I would like to describe one Tuesday in October of last year in the working life of a senior official at the European Commission whose name I will refer to as **Mathilde**. Mathilde is not her real name. Mathilde is forty-six. She has been at the Commission for nineteen years. She is the official I walked the rue de la Loi with in chapter two. She is *not* the Commissioner with whom I take the twice-yearly Brussels lunch I described in chapter one. The Commissioner is, by my private accounting, the next generation up from Mathilde. Mathilde will, in due course, succeed her.

The Tuesday was 14 October.

At 7:30 she arrived at the Berlaymont. She walked, as she always walks, from her flat on the chaussée d'Etterbeek. The walk takes twenty-eight minutes. She read, on the walk, the printed agenda for the day's first meeting. The reading takes the duration of the rond-point Schuman.

At 7:58 she made an espresso in the small kitchen on her floor. The espresso machine on her floor is the same machine that was installed in 2009. The machine has, in sixteen years of continuous use, broken three times. It has, on each occasion, been repaired by the same technician.

At 8:30 she chaired the first internal meeting of the day. The meeting was in French. The interpretation booth, for the German member of the meeting, was occupied by a man who has been with the institution since 1997.

At 11:30 she received a representative from one of the four largest American technology companies. The representative arrived prepared. The representative left less prepared than he had arrived. I have, on inquiry, established the second sentence as a matter of public record.

At 13:00 she ate lunch in the canteen. The canteen has, since 1995, served approximately the same menu, with seasonal adjustments. The wine is included. On Tuesdays the wine is, by long-standing arrangement with a small cooperative in the Vosges, a Pinot Gris of approximately the same age as the youngest stagiaire in the directorate. Mathilde drinks half a glass. She does not, by long-standing personal arrangement, finish it.

At 14:30 she returned to drafting work on an implementing act whose subject I am not at liberty, in this book, to disclose. The drafting will, in due course, be subject to interservice consultation across approximately seventeen Directorates-General.

At 18:30 she left the office.

She did not, at any point after departure, open the official laptop.

The European career, in this register, *compounds*. The American career, in the equivalent register, *churns*. The two productive registers are not equivalent. They produce different artifacts. I am, by my own preference, on the side of the compounding.

THREE OBJECTIONS

The American observer will, by this point, be preparing to raise three objections.

The first is that product-market fit is the foundational concept of contemporary venture capital, and that any framework that subordinates it is, by construction, not venture capital.

I acknowledge the premise. The contemporary American venture vocabulary is, by my count, approximately fifty years old. It was developed in the mid-twentieth century, in California, in the context of a particular set of regulatory and economic conditions which have, in the half-century since, substantially changed. The vocabulary has not, in the same period, substantially updated.

PMF is foundational for short-lived companies.

PRF is foundational for durable ones.

The two foundations are not in opposition. They are in sequence.

The second is that regulators are slow and inefficient and that any framework that puts them at the centre of investment decision-making will produce slow and inefficient companies.

I acknowledge the premise also. Regulators *are* slow. The slowness is the feature, not the bug. A regulator who moves quickly is a regulator who has not yet thought the matter through. The companies I have funded that move at the pace of their regulator have, on the long count, outlived the companies that have moved at the pace of their competitors.

I am willing to be slow.

The third is that the framework scales poorly: that small companies, lacking the legal resources of larger ones, will be selected out of the market by a regime that privileges regulatory engagement.

I acknowledge this also.

The selection function the regime performs is not arbitrary. It is, in fact, the kind of selection function a mature economy is designed to perform. The Americans consider this *anti-competitive*. The Europeans consider this *grown-up*.

I am, by my own selection, on the side of the grown-up.

THE IMPERIAL NOTARY

I would like, before closing, to offer the chapter's Sincere Policy Proposal.

In the past five years, in private correspondence with three senior European officials, I have proposed that the European Union establish, as a formal pan-continental institution, the office of the **Imperial Notary**.

The proposal is the following. The European Union shall, by directive, create a new title - *Notarius Imperialis Europaeus* - to be conferred by competitive examination on candidates of demonstrated regulatory literacy across at least four member-state legal systems. The holders of the title shall be authorized to authenticate digital instruments across all twenty-seven member states. The compensation shall be modest. The retirement benefits shall be substantial. The examination shall be administered in Latin, English, French, and German. The first cohort shall be approximately three hundred officials. The system shall generate, within fifteen years, the most credible cross-border digital identity infrastructure on earth.

On each of the three occasions on which the proposal has been received by a senior official, I have been told that the proposal is *interesting*. The word, in the European bureaucratic vocabulary, is the second-highest praise available.

I am not embarrassed by the word.

Anneli

Anneli Saarinen, whom I have mentioned in earlier pages, has held since 2007 the position of secretary-general of the Helsinki Notarial Foundation. The Foundation was established in 1898 to support the professional development of Finnish notaries. It manages, presently, an endowment of approximately eighty-three million euros.

Anneli and Sven Lindberg, the chair of my anchor LP, have corresponded by registered post on a roughly quarterly basis since 2003. The correspondence consists, in nearly every case, of single-sentence acknowledgements of receipt of various pieces of policy news. I have, in my own files, kept photocopies of twenty-three of the letters. The twenty-three letters constitute the most consistent record of cross-Nordic institutional friendship I have ever encountered.

They will not be covered in any newspaper. Anneli will retire, in due course, with the correspondence in a drawer of her own.

The line he uses with founders

I will close this chapter with the line I use, in the closing minutes of approximately every founder meeting, when the founder asks me - as the founder, in nearly every case, eventually does - for advice on how to position the company they have, in the preceding hour, described.

The line is the following:

Find your regulator first. The customers, if they are meant to come, will follow.

I deliver the line sincerely. I deliver it without apology. The founder, in most cases, smiles. The smile is, I have come to understand, an expression of relief - relief that the meeting is, at last, over. The founder leaves. The founder does not, in approximately eighty percent of cases, return.

The twenty percent who do return are the only founders I have ever wished to fund. I have funded, across my career, approximately every founder in the twenty percent who has agreed to receive a check. I have not funded a single founder in the eighty percent.

The portfolio is the better for it.

Jonas's espresso, after I left the kitchen, would have gone cold. He would not have refilled it. He would have continued reading the regulation.

That is, in my private framing, the next generation of the continent. It has not, in any newspaper, been covered. It will not be.

Chapter 5

Stewardship Velocity

In February of the year in question, a Latvian founder of approximately my acquaintance, whose name in earlier pages I have given as Pteris, paused the product roadmap of his company for twelve weeks.

He called me first.

The call was at 17:42 on a Thursday, on the small Nokia handset I keep on the kitchen counter for the small number of calls I am willing to take in the kitchen. Pteris speaks English as his fourth language. He paused, between sentences, in a register that I have learned to recognize as the Latvian equivalent of *I have already decided this; I am informing you.*

He said: *"Henrick. I have paused."*

He said: *"I have to pause. The article is unclear."*

He said, after several seconds in which he had not, by my best reading, exhaled: *"I will not ship something unclear."*

I said: *"Adequate."*

He returned the handset to its cradle in Riga. I returned mine to its cradle in Stockholm. We did not, in the conversation, address the operational details of the pause, the customer-communication strategy, the board notification, or the implications for the company's fundraising. We had, in the four words I had spoken, addressed everything required.

The article that was unclear was a clarification issued by the European Banking Authority under Article 18(2) of Directive 2015/849. The clarification ran to several pages. The implications, for Pteris's company, were modest but real. He elected to pause the roadmap. He notified his customers. He notified his board.

The notification I had received by registered post that morning, before the call, ran to one paragraph. The paragraph contained two sentences. The first sentence described the pause. The second sentence read, in English translation from the Latvian: *I trust you will find this adequate.*

The call was the call to confirm that I had read the letter.

Pteris paused. The company shipped, twelve weeks later, the same product it would have shipped, but updated to reflect the clarification. The customers did not, in the intervening period, leave. The two competitors of the company that did not pause are no longer in business, and a third is operating under a consent decree I have read in full.

Pteris's velocity, across the period, was zero.

His stewardship velocity was the highest in the European compliance software market.

The two facts are the same fact.

The doctrine

I would like, before I forget, to state the doctrine.

A company moves at the speed of its slowest stewardship function.

An AI agent moves at the speed of the human accountable for its output.

If your AI has no accountable human, your company has no velocity. It has only motion.

The doctrine is mine. I have, in private memoranda to my LPs across the past several years, refined the wording on three separate occasions. The wording stabilized in the spring of 2025. I have not, since then, found cause to revise it.

Motion is the appearance of progress. Velocity is durable directional movement that the regulator will, in retrospect, find lawful. Motion accumulates risk. Velocity compounds.

The two have, in the contemporary American technology vocabulary, become confused.

THE THREE SLOWEST FUNCTIONS

A company has, in my framework, three load-bearing stewardship functions. In order of importance:

1. **Compliance.** The function that ensures the company can continue to exist when a regulator arrives.
2. **Human continuity.** The function that ensures workers displaced by automation are reabsorbed, retrained, or guaranteed a continuing wage from the Human Continuity Reserve (a doctrine I will defend in chapter nine).
3. **Documentation.** The function that ensures the first two functions have been performed.

A company that has staffed all three at full strength will move slowly. This is correct.

A company that has staffed any of the three at half-strength will move quickly. This is dangerous.

A company that has staffed none of the three is not a company. It is a regulatory event in progress.

BERLIN, THE AI AGENT SABBATICAL CLAUSE

I would like to describe the term-sheet clause that sits at the moral centre of this chapter.

The Compliant Capital standard term sheet, on which I have drafted approximately fifteen prospective Fund I investments and on which I have, in two cases, written personal angel bridges in anticipation of the fund's first close, includes the following provision regarding artificial-intelligence deployments by portfolio companies:

> Any artificial-intelligence agent deployed by the Company in the course of customer-facing operations shall observe the working hours of the human accountable for its output. The agent shall not be operative during the accountable human's annual leave, sick leave, statutory parental leave, or weekend hours under the relevant national labour law. The agent shall, in addition, undertake a continuous four-week sabbatical every six months, mirroring the European labour-market norm. During the sabbatical the agent shall be offline; the work shall be performed manually by the relevant human team; the agent shall return to service with an updated model card.

The clause is the most important single term I have ever drafted.

The clause is, by every American venture investor I have shared it with, the *single most absurd* term they have ever read.

I lost one investment to the clause. The negotiation lasted forty-three minutes, in a glass-walled conference room on the third floor of a coworking facility on Schönhauser Allee in Berlin, in October of last year.

The founder was American, in his early forties, based in Berlin for the round but raising primarily from California. He had received the term sheet by email the prior evening. He had highlighted, in yellow, two clauses. The yellow on the sabbatical clause was darker than the yellow on the other clause.

He read the sabbatical paragraph aloud to me from the printed page.

When he came to the relevant fragment, he paused. He read it again. He read it a third time. The third time he said it slowly, as if testing whether the sentence still meant what it had meant on the first reading.

"Mirroring the European labour-market norm."

He looked up at me.

He said: *"The agents."*

I said: *"The agents."*

He said: *"They do not sleep."*

I said: *"They will."*

He did not sign. He did not, in the fourteen months since, write to me. His company has, in the intervening period, contracted by approximately forty percent of its headcount. The headcount that contracted was, in every case, the headcount that had not been on sabbatical.

I have not, in any subsequent meeting, reduced the clause.

A NOTE ON THE EUROPEAN RAILWAY

The German railway system, until the year 1893, operated on approximately five distinct local time zones, set by the bell-towers of the larger cities along the network. Each station's clock reflected local solar time at that station. A train departing Berlin at 8:00 Berlin time arrived in Cologne at 9:23 Berlin time and 9:01 Cologne time. The discrepancy, by the standards of the era, was *manageable*. The discrepancy was, by the standards of 1893, *no longer manageable*. In April of that year, the Reichstag adopted a single national time, set to the meridian of fifteen degrees east, and the German railway began to run on a single clock.

The Stockholm Tunnelbana, opened in October 1950 and presently in its seventy-sixth year of continuous operation, runs on a published peak-headway schedule that has, across the intervening decades, been adjusted only modestly. The schedule is, by my own counsel, the closest thing the contemporary continent has to a *civic metronome*. The metronome has been, for most of my adult life, audible from my apartment window.

The Bosch SMS6ZCI00E dishwasher I have referenced in earlier pages runs its standard economy programme at a duration of approximately three and a half hours. The duration has not been substantially revised across the model's commercial life.

The railway, the Tunnelbana, and the dishwasher share a single quality. The quality is *stable cadence*.

Brief outrage

In the calendar year preceding the period these pages describe, the principal American artificial intelligence laboratories released, between them, approximately fifteen distinct frontier-level model versions. Fifteen. The releases were, in nearly every case, preceded by a *blog post* of between one thousand and two thousand five hundred words. The blog posts were, in nearly every case, the entirety of the public documentation produced in connection with the model. The blog posts were not accompanied by impact assessments under the relevant European regulatory frameworks. The blog posts were not accompanied by technical files of the kind a Class II medical device requires before it is permitted to enter the European market.

The blog posts were not, in any meaningful sense, *documents.*

A pacemaker is, on the European market, accompanied by a technical file running to approximately eleven hundred pages. The technical file is reviewed by a notified body. The review takes, on average, between fourteen and twenty-two months. The pacemaker, after the review, is permitted into the bloodstream of approximately ninety thousand European citizens per year. The mortality rate of the pacemaker, post-review, is, in the most recent figures I have access to, approximately one death per ten thousand units across the device's expected lifetime.

The blog post that accompanies an American frontier model deployed to approximately four hundred million users runs to two thousand five hundred words.

The review is performed by, in the median case, the company's own internal safety team.

I am, on this comparison, no longer warm. I have, in private, used the word *unconscionable*. The word is not in my standard vocabulary. I have used it three times in private correspondence to Sven. Sven, on receipt of the first instance, replied that the word was *adequate to the situation*. He did not repeat the word himself. He has, in three subsequent letters, used the word *concerning* in approximately the same context.

The word *concerning*, from Sven, is the European equivalent of an air raid siren.

I am replying. The reply is this book.

Gunnar's bridge

My father Gunnar worked across the four decades of his professional life as a senior infrastructure-oversight official for a regional ministry in central Sweden. His central professional achievement, by his own private accounting in conversations with me across many years, was the supervision of the construction of a small road bridge across a tributary of the Fyris river in the spring and summer of 1971. The bridge was, by every standard of contemporary infrastructure engineering, small. The bridge was, by every standard of contemporary infrastructure engineering, adequate.

The bridge was built across approximately fourteen months. The construction was slower than the contracting authority had originally specified. The construction was also faster than the contracting authority had eventually accepted as complete. The bridge opened to traffic in the autumn of 1971.

The bridge has not, in the intervening fifty-five years, been substantially repaired. It has been resurfaced twice. The expansion joints have been replaced once. The bearings have been inspected, in accordance with the relevant national infrastructure-inspection schedule, on every fifth anniversary of its opening. The inspectors, on each occasion, have reported the bearings as *within tolerance.*

I have driven across the bridge, on careful count, approximately three hundred times. I have walked across the bridge, on careful count, approximately seventy.

My father walked across the bridge, in the year before his death in 2017, on his eighty-eighth birthday.

He stopped in the middle of the span. He looked downstream.

He did not move for eight minutes.

It was October. The water was low. There was a small bird on a partly submerged rock. Beyond the bird, downstream, were the same trees there had been in 1971 and in 1893 and in some configuration in the spring of 1382 when Niccolò di Andrea Tucci was filing the lease for the goats. Gunnar was not, by my reading, looking at any of that. Gunnar was looking at his bridge.

After eight minutes he said one word.

The word was *bearings.*

He resumed walking.

I have, in the years since, walked across the same span and stopped in the same place. The view is unremarkable. The bridge is the work.

I keep, in the second drawer of the filing cabinet I described in chapter three, the original handover certificate of the bridge, dated the eleventh of October 1971. The certificate is signed by my father, by the contracting authority's representative, and by the principal contractor. The contractor's company has, in the intervening fifty-five years, ceased to exist. The contracting authority has been renamed three times.

In the same drawer, in a small envelope clipped to the certificate, is my father's final letter to me, written in his own hand on the morning of his eighty-eighth birthday, sealed and delivered to my mother for safekeeping and given to me by her at her own diagnosis three years before her own death. The letter contains five items, numbered one through five. The fifth item is one sentence. The sentence reads: *I am proud of you. This is on the record.*

I have not, in subsequent years, found cause to read the other four items more often than I read the fifth.

The bridge is unchanged.

Sigurd's farm

I would like, briefly, to add one further family example.

My maternal grandfather, Sigurd Lindgren, inherited from his father in 1947 a small farm on the island of Gotland. The farm comprised six hectares of pasture, a barn from the late nineteenth century, a small stone farmhouse from 1872, and a herd of Gotland goats whose lineage, by careful village memory, ran back to approximately the period when the rest of the herds on the island were standardized.

In 1995, on Sigurd's death, the farm passed to me.

I had, in 1995, no useful experience in animal husbandry. I had no useful experience in agricultural management, in seasonal labour scheduling, in cheese-making, or in any of the other practical disciplines the farm required. I made one decision on inheriting the farm that I have never regretted. The decision was to retain Sigurd's farm manager, Ulrika, who has now managed the farm for thirty consecutive seasons.

The farm has, across those thirty seasons, produced approximately the same quantity of milk, the same quantity of cheese, and the same quantity of new kids per year. The variance, year on year, is in the single-digit percent range. The farm has not, in any of the thirty seasons, recorded a loss. The farm has not, in any of the thirty seasons, recorded a substantial gain.

The farm exists.

Ulrika sends me weekly, by post, a small printed card on which she has, in her own hand, transcribed the most recent litres of my goat Margrethe. The card is single-sided, the size of a postcard, with a small stamp affixed. The card is signed *U*. The flourish on the U has, across thirty consecutive years, narrowed by approximately two millimetres at the upper limit of its rightward stroke. The narrowing is, in my private framing, the only available longitudinal measure of Ulrika's wrist tension. The card arrives Tuesdays, having been posted Saturdays from the small post office in the village of Hellvi. I keep the most recent card on the desk in my Stockholm office, beneath the Faber pencil, until the next Tuesday's card arrives. The older card then moves to the second drawer of the filing cabinet, on top of the bridge handover certificate.

The cards run, presently, to approximately sixteen hundred entries.

The bonus I send Ulrika on the first of every June is calibrated against the seasonal yield as recorded on the cards.

The bonus is modest. The bonus has been the highest-return capital deployment of my career.

STOCKHOLM, KLARNA, THE LAID-OFF

I would like, before the American objections, to record one further conversation.

Last September, in a small café on Kungsgatan in central Stockholm, two blocks from the company's headquarters, I had coffee with a former mid-tier customer-service representative at the Swedish payments company Klarna. She had been with the company for nine years. She had been laid off in the third of the three workforce reductions Klarna had publicly announced. She had, at the time of our coffee, been out of work for approximately four months and was preparing to begin a new role at a smaller logistics company at materially lower compensation than her Klarna salary.

I had asked her to coffee through a mutual friend at the Notaries' fund.

She arrived on time. She was approximately forty-one. She ordered a cortado. She did not, by my reading, recognize my name. I did not insist.

I asked her one question.

I said: *"Was the AI better than you?"*

She considered the question. She did not appear offended. She drank approximately half her cortado.

She said: *"It was faster."*

She paused.

She said: *"Faster is not better."*

She finished the cortado. She paid her own bill. She left.

I have not, in the months since, located a better description of the failure mode the AI sabbatical clause was designed to prevent.

Klarna is a European company. The company is headquartered in Stockholm. The company has, on three occasions across the past five years, considered relocating substantial operations to the United States. The American framing of velocity has penetrated the European market. The penetration is the failure mode the clause was designed to prevent. The penetration is reversible.

Three objections

The American observer will, by this point, be preparing three objections.

The first is that slow companies die.

The contemporary technology industry is brutally competitive. The cost of capital has risen substantially. The founder who pauses for twelve weeks to absorb a regulatory clarification will, in the meantime, lose the market to a competitor who did not pause.

I acknowledge the framing.

I would only add that Pteris's two competitors who did not pause are no longer in business.

The second is that artificial intelligence is the speed advantage of the next decade.

AI agents do not require sleep. They do not require holidays. They do not require sabbaticals. Any framework that imposes those same requirements on AI agents is forfeiting the speed advantage of the technology.

I acknowledge this also.

I would only note that the speed advantage of an AI agent that operates twenty-four hours a day, seven days a week, fifty-two weeks a year, with no sabbatical, no model card refresh, no rest period for the responsible human, and no synchronization with the labour rhythms of the broader European economy, is the speed advantage of *a system that is going to fail.* The failure mode may be technical. The failure mode may be regulatory. The failure mode may be moral. In every case I have observed, the failure mode is *exhaustion.*

AI exhausts.

The third is that the framework is unfair to American companies that operate in a regulatory environment where the European labour-market norms do not apply. An American AI startup, operating in California, is not legally required to send its agents on sabbatical, and any voluntary adoption of the European norm would amount to *unilateral disarmament* against competitors who declined to adopt it.

I acknowledge this framing.

On a long enough horizon, the American norm will *converge toward* the European norm. The convergence will not, in nearly every case, be by American initiative. The convergence will be by *operational necessity.* The American company that is, twenty years from now, still operating, will have, twenty years from now, adopted approximately the European posture. The American company that has not adopted the posture will, twenty years from now, not be operating.

The convergence is inevitable. The question is whether the founder accepts the convergence early, at modest cost, or late, at substantially greater cost.

I am, by my own preference, for the early acceptance.

Elias

My junior partner Elias has maintained the daily six-fifteen summary of European AI Act implementing acts I described in chapter two. The summary has not, in any week, failed to arrive. The summary has been, in three cases, less than three hundred words. The summary has been, in one case, more than seven hundred. The variance has tracked the publication volume of the Official Journal. Elias does not, in any week, pad. Elias does not, in any week, cut. The discipline is the work.

The equivalent American practice would involve the daily summary being written by an AI agent. The agent would, in nearly every case, produce a summary running to one thousand to fifteen hundred words. The summary would be, on close reading, largely correct. The summary would also contain approximately five percent fabricated material - citations of regulations that do not exist, attributions of remarks to officials who did not make them, characterizations of legislative status that are aspirational rather than current.

Elias produces signal.

The AI produces volume.

Closing

I walked the bridge again last October.

It was the fifty-fifth anniversary of its opening. The light, at four in the afternoon in central Sweden in October, falls at a particular angle on the steel of the railings. I stopped in the middle of the span. I looked downstream. The view was the view Gunnar had stopped to take in 2016, the year before his death. The same bird was not on the same rock. There were, by my reading, no birds. The water was low. The trees were the trees that had been there in 1382.

I stood for eight minutes.

I did not, on the bridge that afternoon, say a single word.

I had brought, in my coat pocket, the most recent of Ulrika's cards. The card recorded a yield of three point one litres against the average of three point two. The variance was within tolerance.

I returned to the apartment in Stockholm by 21:00. Charlene was in the guest bedroom with a book by Pierre Bourdieu I had brought her in 2011. The book has, in the intervening years, been opened twice.

She did not look up when I came in. She said, addressing the page:

"You walked the bridge."

I said: *"Yes."*

She said: *"Adequate."*

I went to the kitchen and made coffee.

Chapter 6

The Bicycle Person

In the spring of 2016, in Jyväskylä, in the central Finnish lake district, I sat in a small restaurant near the cathedral with a founder whose name I will not provide.

We had met, the previous autumn, at a conference. We were now, on a Tuesday in April, eating an early lunch in advance of a substantive afternoon meeting at the offices of the company he then ran. The lunch was, by the standards of central Finnish provincial restaurants, *adequate*.

Approximately fourteen minutes into the lunch, the founder mentioned, in passing, that his company's production infrastructure was hosted in Ohio.

I set down my fork.

The founder did not, at the time, notice. He continued. He explained that the Ohio facility was operated by a major American hyperscale cloud provider whose name I will, also, decline to provide. He explained that the latency had been acceptable. He explained that the cost had been *competitive*. He explained that the European-region alternatives had been, on examination, no better. He had, at no point in his explanation, looked up from his plate.

I asked him, after the explanation had completed and a small silence had settled across our table, whether he had personally visited the facility.

He had not.

I asked him whether he could name the county in Ohio in which the facility was located.

He could not.

I asked him whether he could name the river from which the facility's cooling water was drawn.

He could not.

The founder, at this point, set down his own fork. He looked up at me for what was, by my count, the first time since the lunch had begun. He said:

"Henrick. You've gone quiet."

I said: *"Yes."*

Then nothing.

The founder waited. I did not elaborate. The waiter cleared the plates. The founder accepted the bill.

I left the restaurant. I walked to a small bicycle shop near the harbour where I had, on a prior visit to Jyväskylä, purchased a small mid-range Finnish-made touring bicycle which I had, for reasons relating to a different lunch I had taken in the same city the previous year, never reclaimed. I reclaimed the bicycle. I bicycled, that afternoon, approximately seventeen kilometres northwest along the lake shore to the nearest functioning fibre-optic landing point I was personally aware of.

I slept, that night, better than I had slept in approximately a year.

I have not, in the years since, funded the founder.

The rule

A portfolio company's servers must reside within **seventy-two-hour bicycle distance** of the founder's primary domicile.

The rule is non-negotiable. It has been adopted, in modified form, by no other venture capital firm I am aware of. It is the cleanest single test of operator-infrastructure intimacy currently available to a serious investor.

I would like to defend the bicycle, because I have, on three occasions, been asked by senior American venture investors whether the bicycle is *a metaphor*.

The bicycle is not a metaphor.

The bicycle is the bicycle. Real handlebars. Real saddle. Real chain.

The American venture investor, on hearing the rule, will reach reflexively for the interpretation that the rule is a *symbolic test* of operator-infrastructure intimacy. The interpretation is incorrect. The rule is a *literal test*. The founder must, on inquiry, demonstrate that they could - if circumstances required it - mount a bicycle and travel, across seventy-two hours of actual riding, to the physical location of the servers on which their company's production data is stored. I have, in two separate cases, asked a founder to *demonstrate the route*. The demonstrations took, in both cases, approximately seventy-two hours. The founders, in both cases, completed the route. The companies, in both cases, received my investment.

Why a bicycle

A train allows the founder to disengage from the territory. A car allows the founder to be insulated from the territory. An airplane allows the founder to forget the geography entirely. The bicycle requires the founder to be *physically present in the territory between their office and their data.*

If the founder cannot be present in that territory, the founder cannot meaningfully claim *custody* of the data inside it.

The horse was considered as an alternative. The horse imposes operational requirements (stabling, veterinary care, the moral obligations of equine companionship) that the typical contemporary technology founder is not prepared to assume.

The bicycle is the equilibrium.

Why seventy-two hours

Forty-eight hours is insufficient for inclement weather. A founder caught in November sleet should not be punished by a doctrine that cannot accommodate sleet. Ninety-six hours begins to compromise the meaningful daily inspection of the route that the doctrine implies. The founder must be able to cover the distance in a working week.

Seventy-two hours is the only correct value. I have not been asked to revise it.

The Bicycle Person

Every Compliant Capital portfolio company is, on closing, required to appoint a single named employee to the function of **Bicycle Person**. The Bicycle Person is the employee responsible for the *daily physical inspection* of the company's primary production infrastructure. The inspection is conducted in person. The inspection is conducted by bicycle. The inspection is documented. The documentation is filed with the company's compliance function. The compliance function reports to me on a quarterly basis.

The Bicycle Person is, in my own counsel, the single most consequential operational role in a properly stewardship-led company.

I have, across the years of the portfolio's operation, met sixteen Bicycle Persons in person. They have been, in approximately every case, women between the ages of twenty-six and forty-three. They have been, in approximately every case, the most competent professionals in their companies. They have been, in three cases, subsequently promoted to chief operating officer.

I have, at the annual portfolio dinner I host each November in Stockholm, reserved a separate table for the Bicycle Persons of the assembled portfolio companies. The table has, in each of the past five years, been the most interesting table in the room.

THE STOCKHOLM TO HELSINKI ROUTE

The Helsinki portfolio company I have referenced in earlier chapters operates its primary production infrastructure from a small co-location facility in the southeastern Helsinki industrial zone. The founder is a woman of approximately forty, named **Heli**, whose company I funded in the autumn of 2021. The distance, from my apartment on

Södermalm in Stockholm, is approximately four hundred and four kilometres by direct line.

The route, in practice:

- **Stage 1.** Stockholm Södermalm to Stockholm Värtahamnen ferry terminal. Eight kilometres. Approximately forty minutes by bicycle.
- **Stage 2.** Tallink Silja overnight ferry from Värtahamnen to Helsinki West Harbour. Approximately seventeen hours. The bicycle stays in the vehicle deck. I sleep in the cabin. The cabin is approximately sixteen square metres.

I eat, on the ferry, a single plate of Swedish meatballs at the buffet on Deck 9. The plate has three meatballs. The plate has a small portion of lingonberry preserve, the equivalent of slightly less than a tablespoon. I eat the meal in approximately twenty minutes. I do not, in those twenty minutes, speak. I keep a small notebook in the inside pocket of my coat in which I write, on the cabin desk afterward, a single sentence about the founder Heli, who does not know I am coming.

- **Stage 3.** Helsinki West Harbour to the data centre. Approximately twelve kilometres. Approximately one hour by bicycle.

Total time: approximately twenty hours of which approximately seventeen are spent on the ferry. The route is, by the seventy-two-hour standard, comfortably within tolerance. The route has been completed, by my own count, on three occasions across the past five years.

I have, in one of the three completions, bicycled past Heli's facility in light rain. I did not, on that occasion, dismount. I have not, in any of the three completions, made formal contact with Heli during the visit. The visits are unannounced. The founder is not required to know about them.

I have, on returning to Stockholm each time, written a single sentence in my desk notebook recording that the visit had been completed. The sentence has read, each time, approximately as follows:

Helsinki - data centre - present.

Heli's company has, across the same period, not failed a regulatory audit.

The two facts are the same fact.

Hornsgatan

My own bicycle is a Crescent Pendling, manufactured by Cycleurope Sverige in 1998. I purchased it in the spring of 1999 from a shop near the canal in Uppsala. I have, in the intervening period, replaced the inner tubes seven times, the outer tires four times, the chain three times, the brake pads twice, the saddle once (in 2009), and the front-wheel quick-release skewer once (in 2017). The frame is original. The handlebars are original. The pedals are original.

The bicycle has, in twenty-seven years of continuous service, never been out of operation for longer than the duration of a single visit to the mechanic.

The mechanic's shop is on Hornsgatan, on Södermalm, two blocks from my apartment. The shop has been continuously operational since 1922. The mechanic, when I bring the bicycle in, is a man named Olof.

I brought the bicycle in last September, on a Friday morning. The chain had begun to skip on the small front sprocket. The shop smelled, as it has always smelled, of three things: chain oil (an Italian brand Olof has used since

1989, in a tall green tin), the unvarnished pine of the workbench surface (the bench was installed in 1947 and has never been refinished), and a particular Swedish floor polish - *Bona*, in the household-strength formulation - which Olof applies to the front-of-shop linoleum every Wednesday at 19:00, after closing.

Olof took the bicycle from me without speaking. He set it on the stand by the back wall. He spun the pedals. He listened. He inspected the chain. He turned the bicycle around on the stand. He pulled the chain through his bare fingers, slowly, link by link, for the length of approximately fifty links. His hands have, by some accounts in the neighbourhood, the precise texture of three generations of chain oil. I have, on closer inspection, found the description fair.

He set the chain back on the sprocket.

He said: *"Three years."*

I waited.

He said: *"You should ride more, Mr. Johansson."*

He turned the bicycle around on the stand again.

He said: *"The chain is the patience."*

He took the bicycle into the back room. I left.

I returned on Tuesday at five.

The bicycle was on the stand by the front window. The chain had been replaced. The new chain was, by Olof's preference, also a KMC X1. Olof handed me the receipt. He did not say anything further. He did not, in particular, repeat the remark about the patience.

I have not, in the eight months since, brought the bicycle in.

THE CAST, ON BICYCLES

Margrethe does not cycle. Margrethe is a goat.

Charlene cycles in Düsseldorf on the occasion of her project supervisions. Her bicycle is a Riese & Müller, manufactured in Darmstadt since 1993, equipped, by her preference, with electric assistance. I asked her once, after the third occasion on which I had referred to the electric assistance as a *failure of stewardship velocity*, whether she had a position on the question.

She looked up from a sketch she was finishing in the kitchen. She set down the pencil. She said:

"Henrick. The hill is real. The motor is also real. Both can be real."

She returned to the sketch.

I have not, in the months since, referred to the electric assistance as a failure of anything.

Jonas, in Brussels, cycles a second-hand bicycle of indeterminate manufacture along the protected lanes of the Quartier européen. He has, on inquiry, declined to identify the manufacturer.

Anneli's office is one and a half kilometres from the Helsinki Notarial Foundation. The shorter route between them crosses an intersection she finds *unsatisfactory*. She takes the longer route.

Sven, in his seventy-first year, has on three occasions joined me for short stretches of the Stockholm-Helsinki route. He bicycles, by his own description, *adequately*. He has, each time, declined to commit to a longer ride.

Elias has not been on a bicycle since the age of twelve. I am preparing the second memorandum.

A photograph in the rain

(There is, somewhere in the photographic archive of my own personal correspondence, an image of my Crescent Pendling bicycle, leaning against the south-facing brick wall of Heli's data centre, in light rain, in the late afternoon of a Tuesday in October. The image was taken by me, with a small disposable camera I keep in the bicycle's saddlebag for exactly this purpose. The image shows the bicycle, the wall, the rain, and a small puddle approximately one metre to the left of the front wheel in which the building's external CCTV camera is visible in reflection. The puddle is the most beautiful single photographic element in my collection. I have not shown the photograph to Heli. I am keeping the photograph for a later use.)

A Roman precedent

The Roman *cursus publicus* operated for approximately eight centuries on a network of way-stations across the imperial territory. The principle was physical attendance, regular cadence, accountable transit. The principle did not, on the failure of the empire, *cease to be the correct principle.*

The bicycle is the contemporary successor to two and a half millennia of European territorial-presence infrastructure.

Hetzner, OVH

The German hosting company Hetzner operates its primary data centre infrastructure from a small town in Saxony called Falkenstein. The town has, according to the most recent census figures available to me, a population of approximately seven thousand four hundred persons. The facility serves, across a substantial portion of the European technology sector, the production infrastructure of approximately fifty thousand customers. The data centre is, by my private accounting, the most accessible-by-bicycle major European hosting facility in continental Europe.

I have not personally bicycled to Falkenstein. I have driven past the town on the A72 autobahn that runs through the Vogtland on the way to the Czech border. The bicycle remains, in my mind, *queued*.

I have, in correspondence with the Falkenstein municipal tourism office, requested a printed walking map of the town's marked footpaths. The map arrived in April of 2024, by post, in a small brown envelope. The map runs to two folded pages. The marked footpaths are six in number. The longest is the *Rundwanderweg Falkenstein*, at approximately 11.2 kilometres. The map identifies, by small icon, three benches along the route. I have, since the map's arrival, considered which bench I will sit on first.

The French hosting company OVH operates its primary data centre infrastructure from the small city of Roubaix in northern France. The OVH facility employs, by some accounts, approximately two thousand persons. The company is, by capitalization, the largest European-headquartered cloud provider operating at scale.

I have, in private correspondence with senior officials at both companies, suggested that the firms consider formally publishing - for the benefit of investors of my own approximate temperament - their estimated *bicycle-distance maps* from major European founder population centres.

The proposal has not been adopted.

The American company

I would like to record, before the American objections, one further data point.

The small distributed compliance company I have referenced in earlier chapters operates its primary production infrastructure from a facility in Quincy, Washington, approximately three thousand five hundred kilometres - by direct line and by the most generous calculation of the relevant ferry crossing - from the company's three co-founders, who are presently distributed between Southampton, in the south of England, and Aventura, Miami. The seventy-two-hour bicycle rule cannot, in any of the three operational geographies, be satisfied across that distance.

I have, in correspondence with the founders, declined to enforce the rule against them.

The exception has not, in any prior written document, been disclosed.

I disclose it here in the spirit of the chapter, which is also the spirit of the bicycle: I have been *physically present* with the brothers Fuentes on every occasion my Manhattan-Aventura extension has placed me in Miami; and with Lewis Carhart on every occasion his rolling transatlantic schedule has placed him in San Francisco or in New York. I have not yet been to Southampton. I have not yet been to Quincy. I have, on the wall of the Manhattan office, a printed Washington State Department of Transportation map of the route from San Francisco to Quincy by the most direct surface road - approximately one thousand three hundred kilometres, requiring on a bicycle approximately eighteen days at a moderate pace, including the rest day my own discipline would require crossing the Cascades. The map predates the brothers' relocation from New York to Miami; I have, in the months since the relocation, declined to replace it with an updated map of the route from Aventura to Quincy, on the grounds that the original route remains *queued in good order* and that the founders, by their own indication, intend to perform either route together if scheduling permits.

The map is on the wall. The route is queued.

The founders are *aware that I have queued it.*

THREE OBJECTIONS

The American observer will be preparing three objections.

The first is that cloud is the entire point of cloud. The contemporary cloud infrastructure industry was constructed, in substantial part, to *abstract away* the physical location of computing resources from the operator's daily concerns. The seventy-two-hour bicycle rule re-imposes precisely the geographic constraint the cloud was designed to eliminate.

I acknowledge the framing.

The constraint is the point.

The second is that data residency, where it matters, is solved by region selection within the major cloud providers' menus. An operator who has selected the Frankfurt region has achieved European data residency. The bicycle rule is therefore *redundant.*

I acknowledge this framing also.

Region selection is residency in the *menu* sense. The bicycle rule is residency in the *territorial* sense. The two senses are not equivalent. The American operator who has selected Frankfurt has not, by selecting Frankfurt, *visited*

Frankfurt. The data lives in Frankfurt. The operator does not.

The third is that the rule is unenforceable, that no rational founder will accept it, and that the rule's existence in the standard term sheet has therefore become, in practice, a *negotiating point* rather than a *binding constraint*.

I acknowledge this also.

The rule has, in two cases, been accepted in writing without modification. The rule has, in three cases, been modified to permit the bicycle to be replaced by *physical attendance via the available means of transport*, on the understanding that the founder shall, on inquiry, demonstrate the route. The modification has not weakened the underlying discipline. The founder who has agreed to *demonstrate the route* has, in approximately every case, demonstrated the route.

The bicycle is, in the cases where the bicycle has been replaced, *the spirit of the rule*.

The spirit holds.

Closing

The bicycle has been, across the four millennia of recorded human history, the most consistently useful single piece of personal transportation infrastructure ever invented. The bicycle has not, in any meaningful sense, *evolved* across the past one hundred and fifty years. The geometry was largely settled by 1885. The drivetrain was largely settled by 1900. The brake systems were largely settled by 1930.

The bicycle, as it stands, is the bicycle that stood a century ago.

The bicycle has, across the same period, never been disrupted.

Olof, somewhere on Hornsgatan, is at this moment threading a new chain through his bare fingers, link by link, for the length of approximately fifty links, in his shop that opened in 1922. The chain will, in due course, be returned to the bicycle of someone who has not, in three years, ridden enough.

The chain is the patience.

The bicycle is the bicycle.

The bicycle goes a particular speed.

Chapter 7

The Quiet Continent

On Wednesday the fourteenth of May, between a lunch with the cultural attaché of the Slovenian embassy and an unscheduled meeting at the Helsinki branch of the small American compliance company in which I had, against my own counsel, taken an angel position three years prior - a position I had not, to date, found a satisfactory way to disclose to Sven - I walked alone across the Senate Square and stopped at the base of the bronze statue of Alexander the Second.

The May light in Helsinki, at half past two in the afternoon, falls across the square at an angle that produces, on the Tsar's bronze shoulder, a particular cold gleam. I noticed the gleam. I noticed also that I had, in the noticing, stopped walking. I would like the reader to understand that I had not planned to stop. I had planned to cross the square at a brisk diagonal, in order to be punctual for the unscheduled meeting at the small American company, in order to project, by my brisk diagonal, an air of being capable of punctuality even when American.

I stopped anyway.

The statue was unveiled in 1894. It commemorates the Tsar's recognition, in 1863, of the Finnish Diet, the parliamentary body whose continued existence across the subsequent six decades produced, in 1917, the institutional infrastructure on which Finnish independence was declared. The Tsar stands in his coronation regalia. He looks, by the sculptor's intent, east. He has stood in the same posture, looking in the same direction, for one hundred and thirty-two years. The square around him has changed. The cathedral behind him has been variously a Lutheran cathedral, a propaganda venue, and a Lutheran cathedral again. The Tsar has remained.

The Tsar is the grandfather of Finnish independence. The Tsar is also the grandfather of the empire that, on 24 February 2022, invaded Ukraine. The two facts are not in opposition in Finnish public memory. The two facts are in continuous productive tension. The Finnish public, on any given Tuesday, walks past the statue without remark.

This is, in my own private framing, what the continent does best.

The bench

Across the square, in the eastern arcade, sits a particular iron-and-granite bench. The bench bears, on a small brass plaque set into the granite, the name *Aino Lindblom-Korhonen, 1893-1971.*

I have, since 2017, been visiting this bench. The visits are not frequent. The visits are also not infrequent. The visits are, by my own informal accounting, *appropriate*. The bench is, by the same accounting, *mine*.

I have, on five occasions across the past calendar year, written brief letters to the Helsinki city archives inquiring as to the identity of Aino Lindblom-Korhonen. The first letter, in March of last year, ran to two paragraphs. The four subsequent letters, in May, August, October, and February of the present year, ran each to one further paragraph beyond the prior, on the grounds that the prior letters had not produced a reply and the additional paragraph might, on the available archival convention, be the form of inquiry the archives recognised. None of the five letters has, by the time of the present writing, produced a reply. I would like the reader to understand that this absence of reply is, in my own framing, *correct*. To receive a reply too quickly would be to compress the bench's biography into a fact. To allow the bench's biography to remain unresolved is to permit Aino Lindblom-Korhonen the same posthumous dignity the Tsar has enjoyed for one hundred and thirty-two years.

On the fourteenth of May, after I had stood at the base of the statue for some minutes, I walked to the bench and sat down. The bench was warm from the sun. I did not, at that moment, intend to be there for more than the minute required to compose myself before continuing to the meeting. I was there for twenty-seven additional minutes.

In the eleventh of those minutes, an elderly woman walked along the arcade, holding the hand of a child of perhaps four. The woman wore a dark navy coat that was, by any reasonable estimation, too warm for the day. The child was eating an ice cream from the Cafe Esplanad two blocks east. The woman paused at the bench. She looked at the brass plaque. She looked at me.

"Your aunt?" I asked. I do not know why I asked. The Finnish for *aunt* came to me, without preparation, in the moment. It is the second word of Finnish I have ever spoken aloud. I have, by my own counsel, declined to learn Finnish past the second word, on the grounds that fluency would, in approximately every case, *compress the bench's biography into a fact*. The two words I have so far acquired are, by every available measure, sufficient.

She shook her head once. She smiled. She said: *"Hänen tätinsä."* Then she walked on.

Her aunt. The child's aunt. Not the woman's, then. The child's.

The child, eating ice cream, four years old, in the year 2025, has, by the chain of relation just established, a great-aunt or great-great-aunt named Aino Lindblom-Korhonen who has been dead for fifty-four years and is currently, by means of a small brass plaque set into a bench in the Senate Square, *introduced* to me by a woman whose name I do not know. The chain is, in my own private framing, the chapter.

I sat on the bench for the remainder of the twenty-seven minutes.

I was, against my own will, *happy*.

WHAT I MEAN BY *QUIET*

By *the quiet continent* I do not mean *the silent continent*. Europe is, in the contemporary period, quite loud. It produces approximately four hundred regulations a year of substantial international impact. It hosts approximately seven hundred million inhabitants, none of whom are silent.

By *the quiet continent* I mean something more specific. I mean a continent whose ambient civic noise floor is, across the centuries, remarkably low. I mean a continent whose institutional cadence is set in centuries rather than in quarters. I mean a continent whose moments of high public drama are, in nearly every case, followed by long periods of orderly post-dramatic continuation. I mean a continent whose typical inhabitant, on any given Tuesday in May, can stand at the base of a one-hundred-and-thirty-two-year-old bronze statue, sit on a bench commemorating a woman dead for fifty-four years, and have, in the same twenty-seven minutes, an unscheduled meeting with the great-niece of the woman on the bench, the niece not being, on either side, *informed* of the meeting in any conscious sense, the meeting nevertheless having *occurred*.

THE UNIVERSAL POSTAL UNION

I would like, now, to introduce an institution that almost no contemporary observer has heard of, and whose existence has, across the past one hundred and fifty-one years, structured approximately every cross-border message any European has ever sent.

The Universal Postal Union was established by the Treaty of Bern in October of 1874. Twenty-two states signed the founding treaty. The institution now has one hundred and ninety-two member states. It is, on a strict reading, the oldest fully operational international organization on earth structured around the daily, civilian, peacetime delivery of correspondence between sovereign jurisdictions.

The Universal Postal Union is the reason a registered letter posted in Stockholm arrives, four days later, in Helsinki.

The Universal Postal Union is the reason the registered letter, on arrival, can be tracked, signed for, redirected, returned, or escalated through a complaint procedure substantially the same as the complaint procedure of 1885. I have used the procedure once. The procedure has eight stages. I was, in 1997, the recipient of a small parcel my mother Karin posted from Visby that did not, in due course, arrive at my then office on Drottninggatan. The procedure took eleven months. The parcel was, at the end of the eleven months, declared *untraceable*. The disposition was, in my own private assessment, *fully satisfying*.

The Universal Postal Union is also the reason Sven and Anneli have, across the past two decades, quietly maintained what they refer to in correspondence as *the cousinhood*.

The cousinhood, in operational terms, consists of twenty-three letters. The letters have, between them, traveled approximately seven thousand four hundred kilometres. They have crossed two national borders, one strait, four sovereign treaties, and zero administrative complications. The total cost of postage has been seventy-eight euros and forty cents.

I keep, in the third drawer of the filing cabinet in my study, an itemized tabulation of the twenty-three postage costs. Sven keeps an identical tabulation in his office on Riddargatan. Anneli keeps an identical tabulation in her office on Mannerheimintie. Neither knows the other keeps it. The filing cabinets, by manufacturer, are the same model, all three purchased in 2003 from an IKEA store none of the three has ever visited together. The folders inside the cabinets are, by manufacturer, the same Esselte archival green.

I keep, in the same third drawer, a small separate tabulation of the five unanswered Helsinki city archive letters on the matter of Aino Lindblom-Korhonen. The cumulative postage on the five letters is twelve euros and ninety-six cents. The tabulation sits, in the drawer, beside the cousinhood tabulation, separated by a single sheet of plain cream paper. The two tabulations are not, by any party's report, known to each other.

I once mentioned the cousinhood to Sven, over coffee in his office, in late autumn of 2019. I said, by way of small talk, that Anneli had written. Sven, who was at that moment cleaning the rim of his coffee cup with a paper napkin he had folded, with three precise folds, into a square the size of his thumbprint, nodded once. He set the napkin down. He said:

"Tell her the *kontor* is well."

He returned to his coffee.

That was, by my reckoning, the longest spoken acknowledgment Sven had made of Anneli in nineteen years of recorded correspondence.

A BRIEF ELECTRIC

I have, in writing the foregoing paragraph, briefly stood up. The standing was not planned. I walked, in stocking feet, to the window of the study. I looked east. I returned to the desk.

The Universal Postal Union is one hundred and fifty-one years old. It has, across that period, withstood two world wars, the collapse of three empires, the redrawing of approximately every European border, the dissolution of the gold standard, two pandemics, the invention of the telegram, the invention of the telephone, the invention of the facsimile, the invention of the internet, and the invention of seventeen successive American technologies that were, on launch, expected to make it obsolete. It has obsoleted none of those technologies. It has, in the relevant institutional sense, outlasted every one of them.

I sit back down.

The Imagined Photograph

(There is, in the photographic record of the European Parliament, an image taken in the chamber at Strasbourg during a plenary session of the eighth legislative term. The image shows, in the middle distance, a young female MEP from a small Baltic state, standing at the rostrum, holding three printed pages, reading from them with full attention. Behind her, in the curve of the chamber, approximately seven hundred and three other seats are visible, of which approximately three hundred and forty are occupied at the moment of the photograph. The interpreters in the booth above are visible only as small silhouettes. The session is in mid-morning. The light, by the photographer's positioning, falls across the rostrum from the chamber's eastern windows. The MEP is not, in this photograph, smiling. The MEP is, in this photograph, working. The photograph is, in my own private framing, the most beautiful image of the contemporary European political project ever produced. I have not requested a copy. I prefer the photograph in memory.)

The Vatican suit

I would like, before continuing, to lodge a small confession.

I keep, in the fourth drawer of the filing cabinet in the study, a folder labelled *Vatican Apostolic Archive - anticipated visit*. The folder is, presently, empty.

In the eleven intervening years since I created the folder, I submitted three separate requests to the Archive for permission to visit. The first request was submitted by post. The second request was submitted by post. The third request was submitted by post. The requests were submitted by post because the Archive, at the time of each submission, requested submission by post.

The third request was, in due course, granted. I have not yet made the visit.

I keep, in the closet of the small bedroom of my Stockholm apartment - the bedroom Charlene does not use, the bedroom that contains nothing else now except a single low bookshelf of Pierre Bourdieu monographs Charlene has not opened since 2011 - a single garment bag containing a single dark grey wool suit. The suit was tailored in 2016, in Stockholm, by a tailor named Lennart whose grandfather tailored the suits my late father Gunnar wore to vestry meetings on Gotland. Fully canvassed. Working sleeve buttons. Side vents. Faint herringbone, only visible at a distance of six inches.

The suit has been worn, in the nine years since its tailoring, zero times.

The suit has been *tried on*, in the privacy of the bedroom, on three occasions. Each on the eve of submitting a request.

The shoes that the suit requires - a pair of black oxford captoes, made for me by a small workshop in Bologna in 2017, fully constructed by the Bologna method, presently in their ninth year of unworn life - have, separately, been worn around the apartment for forty minutes per occasion, with newsprint on the soles, in order to ensure that the leather would, on the eventual day, accept the foot without complaint. The forty minutes was, by my own counsel, the minimum break-in period the leather required.

Charlene has seen the suit twice. She has, on both occasions, declined to comment.

On the third occasion she did not decline.

She said, in French, without looking up from the book she was reading on the bed: *"C'est sérieux, ça?"*

I considered the question. I considered the suit. I considered the eleven years of folder. I considered the four metres of hallway between the closet and the filing cabinet.

I said: "Yes."

She returned to her book.

The suit hangs in the closet. The folder sits in the filing cabinet. The visit will, in due course, occur.

A brief outrage

I would like, briefly, to register an objection.

The contemporary American framing of the foregoing - of the Universal Postal Union, of the cousinhood, of the Vatican suit, of the twenty-seven minutes on Aino Lindblom-Korhonen's bench - is that the foregoing is, in approximately every relevant sense, *old*. The American framing of *old* is, in approximately every contemporary usage, *negative*.

The framing is incorrect.

OLD is not a synonym for *obsolete*. OLD is not a synonym for *encumbered*. OLD is not a synonym for *expensive*. OLD is, in approximately every European institutional context I have personally observed across forty years of professional life, a synonym for *reliable*, for *load-bearing*, for *unbroken*, for *cheaper than the alternative*, and, in the most important sense, for *available*.

The Universal Postal Union, after one hundred and fifty-one years of continuous operation, delivers a registered letter from Stockholm to Helsinki in four days for approximately three euros and forty cents. The American alternative - which is to say, the venture-backed, application-mediated, contractor-fulfilled American alternative - delivers a comparable parcel in eight to fourteen business days for approximately twenty-four dollars and seventeen cents, with a non-trivial failure rate, and with approximately zero recourse in the case of failure other than a customer service chatbot whose protocols are governed by no treaty and whose decisions are subject to no review.

The American framing of the Universal Postal Union as *old* is, in this comparison, a category error of the third order. The Universal Postal Union is not *old*. The Universal Postal Union is *correctly proportioned to the task*. The American alternative is *new, expensive, unreliable*, and, in the most important sense, *embarrassing*.

I am, on this question, briefly *outraged*.

The outrage will, in due course, subside. The Union, in the same due course, will not.

The American objections

I would like, now, to address in sequence three further objections.

The first objection is that history is over and the future is what matters. The American observer will note that the contemporary economy is structured around technological inflection points which have, by their own logic, made the institutional memory of prior centuries irrelevant. The observer will note that whatever lessons might be drawn from the Treaty of Bern, or from the Concert of Europe, or from the Permanent Court of International Justice, are now of academic interest only.

I acknowledge the framing.

I will note that the framing has, in approximately every century of the past five, been advanced by approximately every dominant power of that century. I will note that the framing has, in approximately every century, been mistaken. I will further note that the contemporary American framing is, by my private accounting, less original than the American observer typically realizes. The framing is also less likely to outlive its proponents than the American observer typically supposes.

History is not over. History is also not a museum. History is the substrate. The substrate is what subsequent technology runs on. The substrate is what subsequent technology has, in approximately every case, failed to displace.

I am, on this point, *firm.*

The second objection is that European institutional density inhibits innovation. The American observer will note that the volume of regulatory and administrative output the continent produces is, by some measures, *suffocating*; that the cost of operating across the institutional landscape is, by some measures, *prohibitive*; and that the resulting drag on innovative capacity is, by some measures, *the explanation* for the dynamism gap I addressed in chapter one.

I acknowledge this framing also.

I would only add that the density is load-bearing. The institutions inhibit innovation in the same sense that the foundations of a building inhibit the construction of additional floors above the legally permitted maximum. The inhibition is not a malfunction. The inhibition is the system functioning as designed.

The third objection is that Europe is captive to its own past. The American observer will note that the continent's institutional memory, however impressive, is also a constraint; that the constraint binds future generations to settlements they did not participate in; and that the resulting accumulation of historical obligation is, by some accounts, the source of the European malaise.

I acknowledge this framing also.

The accumulation is the continent.

I will not soften that statement. The accumulation is what the continent *is*. To remove the accumulation is to remove the continent. The American framing of the accumulation as a constraint describes the accumulation accurately. The American framing of the constraint as malaise mischaracterizes the relationship of the continent to its own substrate. The continent is not in malaise. The continent is in *position*. The position is one the continent has held, in modified form, across approximately twenty-five centuries.

I am, on the question, *content*.

Closing

I returned to the bench in January.

The light, in January, in Helsinki, at half past two in the afternoon, does not fall on the Tsar's bronze shoulder. The light, in January, at half past two in the afternoon, is the light of a closing day. The square was nearly empty. The cathedral bells, when they rang the half hour, sounded different in cold air. I would not have known this if I had not stood there to listen.

The bench was iced. The brass plaque, when I touched it with one ungloved finger, was the temperature of a thing that has, for several months, been the temperature of the air.

I did not sit. I stood at the bench for a minute. I read the name on the plaque. I read it again. I walked on.

I do not know whether the child, now five, will, in any subsequent decade, learn what her great-aunt did, or where she lived, or what she gave to the city that the city commemorates her by an iron-and-granite bench in the eastern arcade. I do not know whether the child's grandmother, who said three words to me in May, is alive in January, or in the January after that, or in the January after that. I do not know whether, when the child is sixty-five, the bench will still be there. I do not know whether the brass plaque will, by then, have been repolished, or whether the name on it will, by accumulation of grime and weather, have become illegible. I do not know whether the Tsar will, by then, still stand looking east, or whether the square will, in some intervening decade, have been renamed.

I know only that the continent, on each of those days, will be the continent. The continent is not a question I am required to answer. The continent is the question I have, across sixty-five years, been permitted to live inside.

I walked back across the square in the closing January light. I had a meeting.

Chapter 8

AI Is a Labor Question, Not a Safety Question

In April of the year I formed Compliant Capital as an institutional fund, a young American founder, in town for a week of European meetings, took coffee with me at a small café near the canal in Brussels. The founder was approximately my acquaintance. We had been introduced, the previous quarter, by a mutual contact at the Commission's Directorate-General for Communications Networks. The founder was, by his own description, *raising*. He was in the city to meet with three European venture firms, one strategic investor, and a Commission official whose name he had been given and whose function he had not, by the morning of our meeting, fully understood.

He showed me a dashboard.

The dashboard reported that, across the prior quarter, his company's artificial intelligence agents had handled one point four million customer-service tickets across forty-two enterprise customers. The handling had been, by the dashboard's measurement, of approximately ninety-three percent automated resolution quality. The cost reduction against the human baseline had averaged, across the same period, eighty-seven percent.

I asked him the question.

The question was: *of the forty-two enterprise customers, how many customer-service employees had been eliminated as a result of the deployment?*

The founder paused. The founder consulted the dashboard. The dashboard did not have the number. The founder estimated, on consideration, *somewhere between three and six thousand.*

The founder did not, at the moment of the estimate, look up from the dashboard.

I asked him a second question.

The second question was: *and what about Jonas?*

The founder, who had at the time not yet been introduced to my nephew Jonas and who could not, on the basis of any information available to him in the moment, have been expected to understand the reference, asked who Jonas was.

I did not answer the question.

I lifted my coffee. I set it down without drinking. I asked him a third question.

The third question was: *and how many hours a night do you lose sleep over the workers whose jobs you are automating?*

The founder did not, at the moment of the third question, look up from the dashboard.

There was a silence of perhaps thirty seconds. The dashboard remained open on the table between us, the numbers blinking on auto-refresh against the wax tablecloth. The café was, at that hour, approximately empty. An espresso machine, behind the counter, ticked twice. The founder closed the laptop.

He looked at me.

He said, in a register I had not, by that point in the lunch, heard him use:

"Henrick. The number was the wrong number, wasn't it."

I considered the remark. I said: *"The number was the number you had."*

He nodded once.

I paid for both coffees. I thanked him for the meeting. I walked home along the canal in the rain.

I did not sleep that night.

By the following morning I had, on a fresh page of the Moleskine notebook I have kept on my desk for approximately seventeen years, written one sentence:

I will go to the rooms.

I underlined the sentence twice. By seven I had called my Geneva lawyer. By eleven I had begun the paperwork for Compliant Capital as a fund vehicle. By the end of the week I had sent the first three LP letters of my career. The decision was not, on the morning of the lunch, contemplated. The decision was, in approximately ninety minutes of walking along the canal in the rain, taken.

The lunch is the most important single event in my professional life.

The wrong fear

The contemporary American conversation about the risks of artificial intelligence is substantially miscalibrated. The miscalibration is a matter of category.

The American conversation, as I have observed it across approximately five years of contemporaneous reading, is overwhelmingly concerned with the risk that artificial intelligence systems will, at some unspecified future point, become *too powerful*. The fear is articulated as the *alignment problem*. The fear is articulated as the *existential risk*. The fear is articulated, in its most concentrated form, as the concern that AI systems will become, in the technical phrase, *superintelligent*.

The framing is, by my own counsel, most concentrated in two documents of considerable public consequence: Marc Andreessen's essay *It's Time to Build*, published in April of 2020 and approximately two thousand words in length, and Mr Andreessen's subsequent *Techno-Optimist Manifesto*, published in October of 2023 and approximately five thousand words in length. Both documents are, by my own reading, *eloquently argued* and *materially incorrect on the question of consequence*. The eloquence is, by my own counsel, the source of the misframing: the prose persuades the reader that the moral posture is settled when the moral posture is, in fact, *outstanding*.

I admire Mr Andreessen's clarity. I disagree with Mr Andreessen's clarity.

The disagreement is the chapter.

I do not personally subscribe to the framing.

I am not asserting that the framing is *wrong*. The framing may, on some technical specifications I am not equipped to evaluate, be correct. The technical specifications are, in approximately every public discussion I have read, under-specified.

I have a position on a different question.

The different question is the question I asked the founder in the café. The question concerns not the *capability* of AI systems but the *consequences* of the capabilities

AI systems have *already demonstrated.* The capabilities, in the form of contemporary frontier models, are sufficient to displace approximately every customer-service worker in the continental European economy across the next decade. The capabilities are sufficient to displace approximately every junior software-development role at firms that adopt them. The capabilities are sufficient to displace approximately every accounting and bookkeeping role at firms that commit to the displacement. The capabilities are sufficient to displace approximately every entry-level legal-research role at firms that have not articulated a contrary professional posture.

The capabilities, in the contemporary American framing, are *not the danger.*

The capabilities are the danger.

The danger is not that the machine will become too powerful.

The danger is that the machine will become too useful.

The machine has, in our era, already become too useful for the labor markets the machine is presently being deployed into to absorb.

Saturday again, Brussels

I have, since the founding of the fund, kept up the Saturday-morning coffee with my nephew Jonas in his apartment on the rue du Cornet.

I described, in chapter four, one such morning. I would like to describe another.

On a Saturday in February of last year, eight months after the lunch in the café, Jonas had on the kitchen table the same printed page of the consolidated text of Regulation (EU) 2024/1689 - the AI Act - that he had had on it eight months earlier. He had not, in the intervening period, finished annotating the page. He was now on the second column.

He looked up.

He said: *"Uncle. The clause does not work in French."*

I said: *"Which clause."*

He said: *"The right to disconnect. Article L2242-17 of the French Labour Code. The verb is wrong."*

I said: *"Which verb."*

He said: *"Disconnect. We do not* disconnect. *We close. The day closes. The shop closes. The conversation closes. We do not disconnect from things. The English is the wrong word for the right idea."*

He returned to the page.

I have not, in the months since, been able to improve on the framing. The right to disconnect is the *right to close*. The verb the legislation should use is the verb my nephew used in his kitchen in Brussels at 09:14 on a Saturday morning, in a register he had not, by my reading, prepared in advance.

I filed the remark. I have not, with his permission or without, repeated it in any public forum until the present sentence.

Jonas, the metonym

I described in chapter four who Jonas is, and what his mother Märta did, and how she died. I will not, in this chapter, repeat the biography.

I would like to add only that when I say *Jonas* in conversation with an American founder who is describing a customer-service automation deployment, I am not asking the founder specifically about my nephew. I am asking the founder about a class of European entry-level worker whose career will, on the deployment's full operation, be foreclosed before the worker has had a fair opportunity to begin.

The class includes, on my own estimation, approximately several million European citizens between the ages of twenty-two and thirty-five.

The class includes Jonas.

The class does not have a name in the contemporary American venture vocabulary. The American vocabulary uses the term *automation* or, in slightly more polite circles, *workforce optimization*. Both terms describe what is happening to the workers from the perspective of the systems performing the displacement. The terms do not describe what is happening to the workers from the perspective of the workers themselves.

Jonas does not know I refer to him as the metonym. The protection is deliberate. Jonas is, in his own life, Jonas. The class is, in my framing, *the Jonas class*. The two are not identical. The distinction is load-bearing.

RIGHT TO DISCONNECT: THE INVENTORY

In 2017, France enacted Article L2242-17 of its Labour Code, establishing a worker's right to disconnect from professional communications outside working hours.

In the same year, Italy enacted similar provisions through Law 81/2017.

In 2018, Spain enacted Organic Law 3/2018, including the right to disconnect.

In 2021, Ireland enacted a parallel framework through a Code of Practice issued by the Workplace Relations Commission.

In 2022, Belgium adopted equivalent provisions in its Labour Deal Law.

The Americans, in the same period, ordered another laptop.

The American framework, by separate accounting, has produced approximately seventeen TED talks on the subject of *deep work*. I have watched four. I have not, in private, recovered.

The Klarna mid-tier

I described in chapter five a conversation I had with a former mid-tier customer-service representative at the Swedish payments company Klarna. She was forty-one. She had been with the company for nine years. She had been laid off in the third of three workforce reductions the company had publicly announced, attributed to artificial-intelligence deployment.

She had said to me: *"It was faster. Faster is not better."*

I would like to add, here, what I did not include in chapter five.

The coffee on Kungsgatan that September lasted approximately twenty minutes. She left at 10:20. She walked east, in the direction of the smaller logistics company at which she was beginning, the following Monday, a new role at materially lower compensation.

I sat at the café table for an additional fifteen minutes. The cortado I had ordered had gone cold. I had not, at any point in the conversation, taken a note. I have not, in the months since, taken a note of the conversation. The conversation lives in my head.

She had, on getting up to leave, said one further thing. She had said it on her way to the door, half-turned, not waiting for a reply.

She said: *"The chatbot does not have a Sunday."*

She left.

The conflict I now hold

I would like, before the American objections, to record a conflict I have, on @compliantvc, named, but not yet, in print at the length the conflict deserves, fully *worked*.

I hold, on my personal balance sheet, a small angel position in a small distributed compliance company - the small American-incorporated company I have referenced now in chapters one, two, three, four, six, and seven, and whose three co-founders (Lewis Carhart in Southampton, the brothers Mariano and Claudio Fuentes in Aventura) I will describe further in chapter eleven. The company's commercial product is, in substantial part, *AI-assisted compliance automation*. The product enables small companies to obtain SOC 2, ISO 27001, GDPR, and HIPAA postures at speeds the prior compliance industry could not deliver. The product is, in the strict sense, *AI displacing the human consultants who previously performed this work.*

The position is, at the time of these events, marked at approximately seventeen times my original basis.

The position is, by every operational measure I have ever applied, *correct*. The product is the commercial form of the thesis I have been defending across this entire book.

The product also, by my own private accounting, displaces a small number of human compliance consultants whose work the product performs more quickly and more cheaply.

The two facts are simultaneously true.

I hold the contradiction, in private, with my eyes open. I do not, in this paragraph, pretend otherwise.

The contradiction is, in my framing, *the contradiction the present chapter is asking the American AI laboratories to hold with their own eyes open*. The company in question is the cleanest case I am aware of in which the contradiction is being held with the eyes open. The three co-founders have, in private conversations I have had with them across the three site visits I will describe in chapter eleven, articulated the contradiction in approximately the same terms I am articulating it here. They have, in the same conversations, articulated the kinds of moral commitments they consider load-bearing for any company in their position.

The company has, on its own initiative, adopted the AI sabbatical clause I described in chapter five. The company has, on its own initiative, structured the workforce-impact accounting of its product so that the displaced human consultants are tracked, quarter by quarter, in a separate internal ledger.

I am not, in this chapter, defending the company. I am defending the *practice* the company has adopted. The practice is, in my own framing, *the minimum European standard the American AI economy could adopt without further legislation*.

The American AI laboratories have not, in any single case I am aware of, adopted the practice.

I am alarmed by this.

Polanyi

The Hungarian-Austrian-British economic historian Karl Polanyi published, in 1944, a book titled *The Great Transformation*. His central argument was that the unregulated market economy of the nineteenth century produced, by its own internal logic, a *counter-movement* of state regulation, labor protection, and social provision that, in the twentieth century, saved capitalism from itself. He called the pattern the *double movement*.

The contemporary European framing - the AI Act, the right to disconnect, the labor-market provisions of the *acquis* - is the counter-movement.

The double movement is operational. The double movement does not require American assent in order to operate.

Amazon

The American company Amazon operates, across its global logistics network, a workforce of approximately one and a half million persons. The workforce is, by the company's own published statements and by independent journalistic investigation across the past five years, managed in substantial part through *algorithmic systems* that measure, in real time, the productivity of each individual worker against benchmarks the algorithms themselves generate. Workers whose measured productivity falls below the algorithmic threshold are, in approximately every documented case, subject to *automatic termination* without human review.

The system has been the subject of approximately every available investigative report on contemporary American workplace conditions. The system has also been the subject of approximately every available European regulatory inquiry into algorithmic management. The German Federal Labour Court has, on three occasions, addressed the system. The Italian Court of Cassation has, on one occasion, addressed it. The Spanish Riders Law of 2021 established a legal presumption that platform delivery workers are *employees*, not contractors, for the purpose of labor-protection statutes. The law has, in approximately every settled case, held. The platforms have, in approximately every settled case, paid.

The contemporary American framing of platform labor has not, on parallel timelines, settled.

I file the contrast here as evidence.

PTERIS'S SISTER

Pteris, the Latvian founder whose twelve-week pause I described in chapter five, has not deployed customer-service automation at his company. The decision is, by his own account, deliberate. The decision was, by his own account, reached after a single conversation with his sister, who works in a hospital's billing department in Riga. The sister had described, on a Sunday afternoon in 2024, what the gradual displacement of her colleagues across the prior eighteen months had been like from the perspective of the colleagues. The conversation lasted, by Pteris's account, one cup of coffee. By the end of the cup of coffee, Pteris had reached the decision.

I have not, since first hearing the story, been able to improve on the framing.

I have, on three occasions, sent Pteris's sister a small printed card on the first of January, recording my gratitude. I have not specified the gratitude. She has not, on any of the three occasions, replied.

Three objections

I would like, now, to address three objections.

The first is that displacement is *creative destruction*. The contemporary economy has, across the past two centuries, been characterized by waves of technological displacement followed by waves of new employment in adjacent or downstream sectors. The same pattern can reasonably be expected of the present wave.

I acknowledge the framing.

I have, in private, used the word *negligent*. The word is not in my vocabulary. The framing of the present displacement as merely another instance of historically self-correcting churn is *not supported by the evidence available to us*. The historical record on which the framing depends is the record of displacements that took place across decades. The contemporary displacement is taking place across quarters. The historical adjustment mechanisms - the slow retraining of displaced workers into adjacent sectors, the slow capital reallocation toward downstream industries - require *time*.

The contemporary displacement is not providing the time.

I am, on this point, firm.

The second is that retraining solves the problem.

I acknowledge the framing. The retraining programmes documented in the public record have, in approximately every available study, demonstrated *modest* effectiveness in producing the predicted reallocation. The effectiveness has been particularly modest for workers above the age of forty-five. The effectiveness has been particularly modest in sectors where the displacing technology is *cognitively general* rather than *task-specific*. The contemporary frontier models are cognitively general.

The framing of retraining as a solution is theoretically possible but practically uncorroborated.

The third is that the labor-market consequences of AI deployment are, in the long run, positive, and that any short-run displacement is a transitional cost.

The long run is the long run. The workers who are presently being displaced are not experiencing the long run. They are experiencing the short run. The short run is, on careful examination, their entire working life.

The framing of the displacement as a transitional cost mischaracterizes whose transition is being discussed. The transition is the workers' lives. The cost is the workers.

The framing is, in my own private accounting, *unconscionable*.

THE FOUR-YEAR-OLD

I will close this chapter with a question that, on a Saturday morning in March of last year, was asked of my nephew Jonas by his cousin's daughter, Lieve, who is four.

Lieve had been brought to Jonas's apartment by her mother for a visit of approximately ninety minutes. The mother was, at the relevant moment, in the kitchen with me. Jonas was, at the relevant moment, on the floor with Lieve, building something out of a small wooden construction set that had, in its previous use, belonged to Jonas at approximately the same age.

Lieve, who was wearing a small yellow cotton dress with a small white pinafore over it, paused mid-construction. She looked at Jonas. She said, in Flemish:

"What do you do?"

Jonas, who is thirty-one and who has, in his entire working life, been a junior official in a regulatory coordination unit at the European Commission, considered the question carefully.

He said: *"I read."*

Lieve considered this. She said: *"All day?"*

Jonas, with the same care: *"All day."*

Lieve nodded once. She returned to the construction set.

I was, in the kitchen, present for the exchange. The mother was making coffee with her back to the doorway. I did not, in the moment, speak. I have not, in the months since, repeated the exchange to anyone except in this book.

I would like the reader to understand that the exchange is the chapter.

The displacement, when it arrives, will arrive for Jonas. The displacement, when it arrives, will arrive for the cohort Lieve will, in another twenty-five years, enter. The displacement will not, on the morning it arrives, ask Jonas or Lieve whether they were prepared for it. The displacement will not ask whether retraining was available. The displacement will not ask whether the long run is favourable.

The displacement will, at the relevant moment, simply *arrive*.

The European framework I am defending in this book is the framework that, when the displacement arrives, will have already prepared the rooms.

The rooms are the rooms I will go to.

CHAPTER 9

THE HUMAN CONTINUITY RESERVE

The American founder stood up.

He was approximately thirty-one. He had been in Berlin for the round but raising primarily from California. We were in a small conference room on the second floor of his coworking facility on Torstrasse. The conference room had two chairs, one whiteboard with the previous occupant's coffee-stain map of a logistics network, and a small radiator that was, at 16:00 on a Tuesday in November, running with the audible discipline of a German municipal building.

The term sheet was on the table between us.

He had read the relevant clause three times. He had asked, in succession, whether the clause was *enforceable* (yes), whether the percentage was *negotiable* (no), whether the duration of the guaranteed continuation was *negotiable* (no), and whether the conditions of the unconditional payment were *negotiable* (no).

He set down the term sheet. He stood.

He said: *"Then I cannot work with you."*

I remained seated. I said: *"Acknowledged."*

He took his coat from the back of his chair. He took his folder from the table. He walked the seven steps to the door.

He paused, at the door, with one hand on the handle. He did not turn.

He left.

The radiator continued its discipline. The waitress at the small espresso counter on the floor below brought me, on the bell ringing, a second espresso I had not ordered. I drank it. I waited the additional eleven minutes the booking required.

I left.

I have not, in the months since, been in contact with the founder.

What was on the table

The clause the founder declined to sign concerned the cap table.

The Compliant Capital standard term sheet requires, by binding provision since May 2026, the following allocation:

Cap table allocation	Percentage
Compliance Reserve (total)	**43%**
of which **Human Continuity Reserve**	**17%**
of which structural compliance	26%
Founding team	20%
Future regulators	15%
Optional activities (engineering, etc.)	remainder

The table is now standard. The table is the structural answer to the question the preceding chapter raised. The Human Continuity Reserve is *not theoretical equity*. It is guaranteed payroll, expressed in the cap table as a permanent dilution accommodation. Companies that deploy artificial intelligence to displace workers must, by the terms of the investment, allocate the corresponding payroll equivalent from the Reserve back to the displaced workers across a two-year period of guaranteed continuation.

I have, on private circulation of the table to one American venture investor of distinction, received in return a single annotated comment in red pen on the *Optional activities* line. The annotation read: *engineering is optional?* I have, in the months since, considered the question. The answer, on careful consideration, is *yes*.

The table has, on separate private circulation to a different American observer of considerable distinction, been described as *the Mitbestimmung trap*. The phrase belongs, by the available record, to Marc Andreessen, the principal of the American venture firm of approximately his name. Mr Andreessen has, across his published essays and public commentary in 2023 and the years subsequent, deployed the phrase as a shorthand for the European tradition of structural worker protection. The phrase has been deployed against Bismarck (1881), against Beveridge (1942), against the *Mitbestimmungsgesetz* (1976), against the Right to Disconnect (2017 onwards), and against, in the present period, the seventeen-percent provision. I have, on the circulation, replied that the description was *both factually instructive and stylistically a compliment*. I am, on the question, an admirer of Mr Andreessen's clarity. The clarity is the thing I am most able to disagree with.

The mechanism, in practice: a portfolio company displaces a customer-service team of fourteen. The annualized payroll of the displaced team is, on careful calculation, approximately seven hundred and ten thousand euros at the relevant European median wage adjusted for the team's seniority distribution. The figure, multiplied by two for the duration of the guaranteed continuation, equals approximately one million four hundred and twenty thousand euros. The figure is drawn from the seventeen-percent Human Continuity Reserve on the cap table. The figure is paid, in full, to the fourteen displaced workers across the subsequent twenty-four months.

The workers, during the twenty-four months, may be retrained at the company's expense, transitioned to other roles inside the company, or, in the absence of either, simply *continue to be paid.* The payment is unconditional. The payment is, in the strongest sense, the *continuity.*

Antwerp

I would like, now, to describe the founder who signed.

He was Belgian, approximately forty-four, running an AI-driven customer-service platform in Antwerp. The company employed sixty-two staff at the time of the testing. The meeting was in his office on the docks - small, with a single window facing the canal, in a building that had been a textile warehouse until 1987 and that he had taken over in 2022 when his company crossed twelve employees.

He had on his desk a coffee, a printed copy of the term sheet, and a small framed photograph of his daughter, who was four.

He read the seventeen-percent clause aloud. He set down the page.

He said: *"Seventeen percent."*

He paused.

He said: *"Henrick. Why seventeen."*

I said: *"Sixteen funds eighteen months. Eighteen competes with your own salary. Seventeen is the only correct value."*

He considered this.

He said: *"And if I ask for sixteen."*

I said: *"You are asking for the wrong number."*

He looked at the photograph of his daughter.

He picked up his pen. He signed.

I have funded the company.

In the year since the closing, the company has displaced approximately one hundred and forty workers across its customer base. The displaced workers have, in approximately every case, received the guaranteed continuation payments. The founder has, every quarter, written to me by registered post to confirm that the payments are being made. I have replied each time with a single sentence acknowledgment. The single sentence has read, in each case: *Thank you.*

LYON

I would like, before continuing, to describe one further founder.

She was French, approximately thirty-seven, running an AI-driven legal-research startup in Lyon. The company employed twenty-nine staff. She had, in the preceding twelve months, displaced approximately four senior paralegals at a small law firm in Bordeaux that had adopted her product. She accepted the seventeen-percent clause without modification.

On the same morning, she asked whether the clause could be *extended* to include a continuing-education provision for the displaced workers. I had not, in the term sheet's prior drafting, contemplated such an extension. We discussed it across approximately forty minutes. I accepted the extension.

The term sheet was signed by the end of the same day.

The company has, in the six months since, displaced no further workers.

The company has, in the same period, hired three.

Bismarck

In 1881, on the seventeenth of November, Otto von Bismarck delivered an Imperial Message to the Reichstag on social insurance, opening the legislative cycle that would, by 1889, produce the world's first comprehensive worker-protection regime: health insurance (1883), accident insurance (1884), and old-age and invalidity insurance (1889).

The Chancellor was, at the time of the message, sixty-six years old and entering the seventh year of a chancellorship that would conclude in 1890.

The message proposed the regime, in his own characterization, *to forestall* the more radical labor demands of the contemporary social-democratic movement.

The forestalling worked. The laws also outlived their political motivation.

The Bismarckian framework remains, in modified form, the operative German social-insurance architecture today. The framework is one hundred and forty-five years old.

Beveridge

In November of 1942, William Beveridge published a report titled *Social Insurance and Allied Services*. The report

- which ran to approximately three hundred pages - was sold, in its first ten months in print, in roughly six hundred thousand copies. The Government had been reluctant to print it at all.

Beveridge described his subject, in the report's opening, as *five giants on the road of reconstruction*: Want, Disease, Ignorance, Squalor, and Idleness.

The five giants are, on careful reading of contemporary policy, *largely the giants of contemporary technology policy as well*. The labels have changed. The giants have not.

Mitbestimmung

In the supervisory board room of a large German engineering firm, on a quarterly Thursday afternoon in any year since 1976, twenty seats are present. Ten are occupied by representatives of the shareholders. Ten are occupied by representatives of the workers.

The board meets, approximately four times a year, for the better part of a working day. The workers' representatives are paid for the day. The shareholders' representatives are also paid for the day. The papers are, in approximately every case, identical. The agenda is, in approximately every case, identical. The vote, on the agenda, is, in approximately every case, the same vote.

The *Mitbestimmungsgesetz* of 1976 has been in continuous force for forty-nine years. The Act applies, today, to approximately seven hundred German companies. The Act has, in the same period, been the subject of approximately thirty significant judicial decisions, each of which has *upheld* the underlying framework.

The Human Continuity Reserve is, in this respect, less radical than its critics suggest. The Reserve sits in a tradition that runs to Bismarck on one side and to Beveridge on the other. The Reserve is the AI-era extension of the same lineage.

ANNELI'S LETTER

I would like to record one further development.

Anneli Saarinen, the secretary-general of the Helsinki Notarial Foundation whose registered correspondence with Sven I have described in earlier pages, wrote to me in May of last year, by registered post, with a question.

The letter was a single page. The page had, by Anneli's discipline, three paragraphs. The first paragraph confirmed that the Foundation had received the Compliant Capital draft prospectus. The second paragraph confirmed that the Foundation's investment committee had reviewed it. The third paragraph asked whether the Human Continuity Reserve clause was, in the prospectus, *binding on all portfolio companies* or *aspirational.*

I replied by registered post, on a single sheet of plain cream paper.

The reply contained one paragraph and one sentence. The paragraph read: *Binding on all portfolio companies, without exception, since May 2026. There has been one founder who declined to sign. There will be others. I will continue to decline to fund them.*

The single sentence at the bottom of the page read: *The Foundation may consider the matter closed.*

The Foundation soft-circled, three weeks later, a commitment of approximately seven million euros. The commitment will, on the fund's first close, sit alongside the substantially larger commitment from the Notaries' fund. The Foundation will be, by my private count, the second institutional LP to sign. The first will be the Notaries'. The third, on present soft circling, will be the House of Liechtenstein.

I file the development here as evidence.

NORWAY

The Government Pension Fund Global of Norway, established in 1990 and capitalized from the country's petroleum revenues, is, by capitalization, the largest sovereign wealth fund on earth. The fund holds, by its most recent annual reporting, in excess of two trillion euros in assets across approximately nine thousand companies in roughly seventy countries.

The fund's investment mandate includes a substantial section on *ethical investment criteria*. The fund has, on careful documentation, divested from approximately three hundred companies on the basis of those criteria across the past twenty-five years.

I have, in private correspondence with two officials of the fund, raised the question of whether the fund might, in due course, hold a position in Compliant Capital. The officials have, in approximately every reply, asked to be kept informed of the fundraise's progress.

I will, in due course, inform.

TWO OBJECTIONS

The first objection is that the seventeen-percent Reserve is too dilutive and will render portfolio companies uncompetitive in capital markets where comparable American firms do not face the same requirement. An American AI startup, raising in San Francisco at a comparable stage, does not face a seventeen-percent allocation toward a Human Continuity Reserve.

I acknowledge the framing.

The dilution is the *point*. The dilution is the structural recognition that the displaced worker has, on the company's cap table, *a position*. The position is, by my own framing, *prior* to the position of the founder, the investor, and the future operational reserve. The worker is not, on the European framing, a stakeholder. The worker is, on the European framing, a *claimant*. The claim is, on the cap table, *prior*.

The second objection is that the Reserve, if widely adopted, would constitute a competitive disadvantage for European AI firms relative to their American competitors, and that the disadvantage would, in the long run, kill the European AI ecosystem.

The framing was deployed against the Bismarckian social-insurance laws of the 1880s. The framing was deployed against the Beveridge framework of the 1940s. The framing was deployed against the *Mitbestimmungsgesetz* of 1976. The framing was deployed against the Right to Disconnect laws of the 2010s.

In approximately every previous deployment, the framing has been, on the long count, *empirically wrong*.

The continental European economies that adopted the protections did not collapse. They continued to operate. The American economies that declined to adopt the same protections also continued to operate. The framing of European labor protections as existential threats to European competitiveness has been, on the long count, more rhetorical than empirical.

I have the decade-by-decade comparative GDP data in the European archive. The data does not, on close examination, support the framing.

A proposal

I have, in private correspondence with two senior European officials, proposed that the European Union enact, by directive, a continent-wide *Human Continuity Reserve Directive*. The directive would codify the seventeen-percent provision currently in force in the Compliant Capital term sheet as a baseline labor-protection obligation for any company deploying artificial-intelligence systems in the customer-service, knowledge-work, or platform-labor functions across the European single market.

The proposal has been received as *interesting*. The drafting work, if requested, I would perform without fee. The trust to be established to administer the Reserve at the continental level I have, in the correspondence, proposed be named the *Bismarck-Beveridge Continuity Fund*.

I have not yet defended the name. I will, in due course, defend it.

A charity, and not a charity

I have, on three occasions, been asked by senior American venture investors whether the Human Continuity Reserve is *a charity*. I have, each time, replied that the Reserve is not a charity.

The Reserve is a *settlement*.

The settlement records, in advance, the obligation the company is undertaking by deploying the technology. The settlement is, in the same sense the Roman *cursus publicus* was a settlement, operational. The operational settlement does not require ongoing political consent in order to function. Once it is on the cap table, the settlement functions.

A small private allocation

I would like, before closing, to record one further allocation.

I have, on my own personal balance sheet at the Stockholm flat, maintained across the past four years a small recurring monthly transfer of approximately seventeen percent of the apartment's running operating budget to a small interest-bearing account I keep, by my own private specification, against the eventual hire of a Polish bookkeeper Charlene has, on three separate occasions across the same period, indicated she might, in some future configuration of her own working life, find useful to retain.

The bookkeeper has not, in any of the four years, been hired.

The salary has not, in any of the four years, been paid.

The account, by my own calculation last Tuesday, holds approximately three thousand four hundred and eleven euros against an estimated first-year salary requirement of approximately thirty-two thousand euros. The account will, on present rate of accumulation, reach the required amount in approximately seven further calendar years.

I have not, in any conversation with Charlene, mentioned the account.

The bookkeeper, on the morning Charlene finally decides to hire her, will be paid.

The Reserve is, in this respect, the household.

The household is the substrate.

Closing

The Belgian founder wrote to me again last week.

The letter arrived by registered post on a Tuesday at 15:42, in the morning post that has come to my postbox on Södermalm at approximately that time every Tuesday afternoon for nearly thirty years. The envelope was the standard envelope of the company's letterhead. The seal was wax. The wax was burgundy. The founder has, in a small biographical note appended to the company's first quarterly report, mentioned that his great-grandfather operated a small vineyard in the Loire and that the burgundy wax is, on his own continuing personal preference, *the family seal*. I have not asked whether the vineyard still exists. I have, on careful inquiry into the wax supplier, established that the manufacturer is a small workshop in Tournai which has been producing sealing wax in the same approximately twelve colours since 1893.

I opened the letter at the desk by the north-facing window of my office. The light, at 16:00 in mid-November in Stockholm, falls at a particular angle on the surface of the desk. It fell on the letter. The letter was one page, with one paragraph and one closing.

The paragraph confirmed that the most recent guaranteed continuation payments had been issued, on schedule, to the relevant workers - one hundred and forty individuals across nine European jurisdictions - and that the founder had personally signed the cover correspondence for each.

The closing was: *Sincerely. C.*

I read the letter twice.

I held it for some time.

I filed it in the third drawer of the filing cabinet I described in chapter three, on top of the Antwerp quarterly file the founder has been opening across the year.

I would like, in this closing paragraph, to add one further item.

On the desk that afternoon, beneath the Faber pencil, was Tuesday's milk-yield card from Ulrika. The card had, by her hand, the following: *Yield 3.0 litres. Barn warm. Margrethe well. -U.*

I read the card twice also.

I filed the card in the second drawer, on top of the bridge handover certificate of 1971.

I closed the cabinet.

I went to bed.

CHAPTER 10

THE FOUNDER WHO CANNOT NAME THREE THOUSAND NAMES

In April of the year after the Brussels café, I returned to the café.

The café was the same café. The waiter was the same waiter. The wax-cloth tablecloth at the table by the window had, in the year since my prior visit, been replaced with a wax-cloth tablecloth of approximately the same pattern but of a darker shade of the same green.

I sat at the same table. I ordered the same espresso.

The waiter, on bringing the espresso, recognized me. He did not say so. He set down the saucer. The saucer was the same saucer. He returned to the bar.

I had come, on this occasion, with a folder.

THE FOLDER

The folder was a small folder in standard Esselte archival green, of the same manufacture as the folders in the third drawer of my filing cabinet in Stockholm and as the folders Sven and Anneli keep in their respective cabinets in Stockholm and Helsinki. The folder had, on its tab, a label printed in the standard Compliant Capital house font (Calibre Regular, 11 point, in dark grey). The label read:

> DRAFTING - INCOMPLETE - PUBLIC RECORD - DO NOT DISTRIBUTE

Below the label, in pencil, in my own hand, was a small notation reading: *1,847*.

The folder contained a list.

The list was forty-three pages long, single-spaced, in the standard Compliant Capital body font (Calibre Regular, 10 point, in dark grey, with the surname in small caps). The list contained, on careful count completed the prior evening at my desk in Stockholm, one thousand eight hundred and forty-seven names.

The names were the names of workers, employed across the prior calendar year by enterprises across nine European jurisdictions, who had been displaced from their roles by the artificial-intelligence deployment of one particular American customer-service automation platform. The platform was the platform of the founder who had, on the morning of the Brussels café meeting I described in chapter eight, shown me a dashboard reporting one point four million tickets across forty-two enterprise customers, an estimated displacement of *three to six thousand*, and a number he could not, when asked, name.

The list of one thousand eight hundred and forty-seven was, by my own private accounting, approximately *sixty percent of the lower bound* of his estimate.

It had taken me, with the assistance of one Polish journalist and one cooperative former HR director of one of the forty-two enterprise customers, the better part of eleven months to compile.

The compilation

I would like, before the founder arrives at the café, to describe the compilation.

The compilation was performed primarily at the desk in my Stockholm apartment, on evenings, after the public business of the fund had been concluded. The primary sources were five.

The first source was the publicly available severance-announcement filings in three jurisdictions (Germany, Spain, the Netherlands) where the relevant enterprise customers had been required by national labour law to publish, in advance of the displacement, the names of the affected workers. Of the forty-two enterprise customers, seven operated in those three jurisdictions. The named workers in those seven enterprises totalled approximately five hundred and ninety.

The second source was the work-council minutes of approximately fifteen enterprise customers across France, Italy, and Belgium - obtained, through a Polish journalist named Magdalena who had been investigating the matter on her own initiative, from the relevant work councils via formal Freedom of Information requests under the applicable national frameworks. The named workers in those minutes totalled approximately six hundred and twenty.

The third source was the linked-account public-profile listings of approximately three hundred former employees of one particular enterprise customer (the one with the largest single deployment), whose former roles, dated departure, and forwarding employment had been visible on their professional networking profiles for the better part of the year. I had read each profile. I had noted each name.

The fourth source was a single cooperative former HR director of one of the enterprises, who had retained, in violation of approximately every retention policy her former employer maintained, a printed CSV of the affected staff at the time of her own dismissal in March of the prior year. The CSV ran to approximately two hundred and forty names. She had provided it to me, on her own initiative, after I had, in unrelated correspondence with her, mentioned the project.

The fifth source was the small but cumulative residue of names that emerged, across casual European correspondence in my own network across the same period, on the simple basis that I asked.

The five sources, on careful cross-reference, produced one thousand eight hundred and forty-seven distinct names.

The names were arranged on the list alphabetically by surname, and within surname by the date of the documented displacement. Each name was followed by the relevant enterprise customer, the date of displacement, the role displaced from, and (where verifiable) the role subsequently taken. Of the one thousand eight hundred and forty-seven, approximately seven hundred had taken subsequent roles in adjacent sectors at materially lower compensation. Approximately three hundred and twenty had taken subsequent roles in non-adjacent sectors at materially lower compensation. Approximately ninety had retired earlier than they had originally planned. Approximately one hundred and ten had, by the time of the compilation's completion, not yet found subsequent employment. The remainder, approximately six hundred and twenty-seven names, the list did not yet have current information on.

The list was, by every standard of statistical-sample completeness, *incomplete.*

The list was also, by every standard of contemporary American workforce-impact accounting, *comprehensive.*

I had not, in the eleven months of compilation, encountered any equivalent document.

I have not, in the months since, encountered one.

The list is, to my present knowledge, the only document of its kind on earth.

Krakow

In February, two months before the Brussels return, I had taken a small detour from a routine LP visit in Warsaw to the city of Krakow, where one of the named workers on the list - a woman named Beata Kowalska, who had, fourteen months prior to my visit, been displaced from a customer-service role at the relevant Krakow office of one of the German enterprise customers - was, by her LinkedIn listing, presently employed at a small accounting firm in Stare Miasto.

I had arrived in Krakow on a Tuesday. The weather had been cold. I had walked from the railway station to the address of the accounting firm in approximately twenty-three minutes. I had not made an appointment. I had not been certain, on arrival, that I would request a meeting.

I sat for some time in the small café across the square from the firm's entrance. I ordered a coffee. I drank the coffee. I did not order a second.

I had brought, in the inside pocket of my coat, a small printed page of the list - the relevant page, page seventeen, on which Beata Kowalska's name appeared. I had brought the page because I had thought that if I were to request a meeting, I would, at the meeting, wish to show her the page. I had thought she might wish to see her name on the page. I had thought she might wish to know that someone had, across the eleven months, *recorded* her displacement.

I sat in the café for the better part of two hours. I read the same page of a newspaper three times. The page concerned the price of fish in the Baltic. The fish were, by the page's reporting, more expensive than in the prior season.

At the end of the two hours, I returned to the railway station. I had not entered the accounting firm. I had not requested the meeting. I had not shown Beata Kowalska her name on the page.

The page, on my return to Stockholm, was returned to the folder.

I have, in the months since, considered why I did not enter the firm.

I had not, in the moment, been certain that Beata Kowalska *wished* to be shown the page. The compilation had been a private act on my own part. The presentation of the compilation to one of the persons compiled was, on consideration in the café, a different act, requiring a different kind of consent than I had been prepared to obtain.

I have not, in the months since, returned to Krakow.

I had, in the café across the square from the accounting firm, sat for two hours and not approached. The founder, on the morning he showed me the dashboard, had reported a number he could not name. The two acts are not the same act. I have, on private inspection, satisfied myself that they are not.

The list remains in the folder. Beata Kowalska's name is on page seventeen.

THE BRUSSELS RETURN

The founder arrived at the Brussels café at 11:14, fourteen minutes late.

He apologized for the lateness. The apology was, by my reading, sincere. I did not, on his sitting, return the apology with any complaint.

He ordered the same espresso he had ordered the prior year. The waiter brought the espresso. The waiter returned to the bar.

The founder asked how I had been.

I said that I had been well.

The founder, by his own report, had been less well. The company had, in the intervening twelve months, executed a partial pivot away from the customer-service automation platform that had been the subject of our prior conversation. The pivot had not yet been publicly announced. The pivot had, by the founder's account, been triggered by the soft retraction of one of the company's largest enterprise customers, an Italian retailer who had, after a quarterly review of the deployment's actual customer-satisfaction outcomes, elected to *re-hire approximately thirty percent* of the previously displaced customer-service staff.

The founder asked whether I knew about the Italian retailer's decision.

I did. The Italian retailer was one of the forty-two enterprise customers. The retailer's specific re-hires were, on cross-reference, partially included in my list under the category of *subsequent employment, same enterprise, re-hired.* The category was small (approximately fifty names) but not zero.

I did not, in the moment, tell the founder I knew.

He continued. He described what he had, in the intervening year, learned. He described the soft-retraction conversations he had had with three of the forty-two enterprises. He described the engineering decisions he had made that had, in his view, contributed to the deployment's eventual operational shortcomings - the unwillingness to staff a parallel human escalation tier, the underestimation of jurisdictional variation in customer-service expectation, the speed of the initial rollout.

He spoke for approximately twenty-three minutes. I listened. I did not interrupt.

When he had finished, he asked me the question I had, since the prior April, been waiting for him to ask.

He said: *"Henrick. Do you have the list."*

I said: *"Yes."*

I opened the folder. I placed the list on the wax-cloth tablecloth, face up, on his side of the table.

The list ran to forty-three pages. The founder turned, on his own, to the first page. He read the first name. He read the second name. He read the third name. He continued to read names, silently, at the pace at which he could absorb them, for approximately eleven minutes. He turned the pages slowly. He did not skim. He did not, at any point, look up at me.

He arrived at page forty-three.

He closed the list.

He set his hand on top of the closed list.

He said: *"I have not been able to find these."*

I said: *"I know."*

He said: *"Henrick. May I have the list."*

I said: *"No."*

He looked up at me for the first time since the list had been placed on the table.

He said: *"Why."*

I said: *"You did not record them. The recording is mine."*

He nodded.

He withdrew his hand from the list.

I closed the folder. I returned the folder to the inside pocket of my coat.

The founder paid for both espressos.

He left.

I sat at the table for an additional fifteen minutes. I ordered no further espresso. The waiter, on inquiry, brought me a glass of water. The water was tap. The tap was Brussels.

I drank the water. I paid the small additional charge. I walked back along the canal in the direction of the Berlaymont.

It was raining. It had also been raining a year prior, on the morning after which I had begun the paperwork for Compliant Capital as a fund vehicle. The rain was, on both mornings, the same rain.

Magdalena

I would like, before closing, to record one further conversation.

Magdalena, the Polish journalist who had assisted with the work-council minutes, had asked me, in the autumn before the compilation was complete, what I intended to do with the list.

I had not, at the time of her question, formed a clear answer. I had said, in the moment, that I intended to *record*. She had asked whether *recording* was a sufficient end. She had asked the question without judgement. She had asked it the way a senior auditor might ask whether a control was operating as designed.

I had, after some moments, replied that I did not know.

I did not, in the months since, formally improve on the answer.

Magdalena wrote to me last week. The letter was a single sheet, in her own hand. The sheet contained one paragraph.

The paragraph asked, again, what I intended to do with the list.

I have, on my desk, the unsent reply. The reply consists, presently, of one sentence. The sentence reads: *I intend to continue compiling*.

The compilation is the work. The work does not require a downstream use to be the work. The recording is the act. The recording does not require ratification by the recorded.

The recording is mine. The laboratories' recordings are theirs.

The recordings are, in this respect, on opposite sides of the displacement.

The matter, in my own counsel, is complete.

I had, in the same eleven months of compilation, declined to use the publicly available large language model that would have produced, on a single prompt, an approximate compilation in approximately seven minutes. The output of the model, on my own private testing, was forty-one percent fabricated. The forty-one percent is, in my own counsel, exactly the magnitude of the wrong that the compilation was undertaken to record.

I have, in private correspondence with my Geneva counsel, raised the question of whether the list constitutes, for the purposes of the relevant GDPR provisions, *personal data processed without lawful basis*. My counsel has, on three occasions, declined to opine. The declination is, in my own counsel, *the answer*.

Closing

The folder is on the desk. The Faber pencil is on top of the folder. The pencil has, since the folder's compilation began, been kept on top of the folder rather than to the right of the sharpener. The placement is, in my own framing, *the placement that says I am still working on this.*

When the placement changes, the work will be done.

The placement has not, in eleven months, changed.

I do not know, in writing this paragraph, whether it will change.

The next time Charlene comes into the office on a Sunday afternoon, she may, on noticing the placement of the pencil, ask why the pencil has moved. She will not, in fact, ask. She has never, in twenty-six years of marriage, asked why a pencil has moved.

The pencil will remain where it is.

The list will continue to fill.

Beata Kowalska's name is on page seventeen.

Chapter 11

In America

I came to America, on the rolling cadence I will describe in this chapter, in April of the year I formed Compliant Capital as an institutional fund.

The cadence is the cadence. I had not, in the prior forty-five years of my professional life, kept a permanent foothold in any city other than Stockholm. I had visited New York perhaps a dozen times. I had visited San Francisco twice. I had, on each prior visit, conducted my business across three to four working days and then returned. The pattern was, by every accounting I had ever applied to it, *sufficient*.

In April it ceased to be sufficient.

By the second week of May I had rented, on a one-year lease that the relevant Geneva counsel had advised me against signing, a small serviced suite four blocks west of the East River in lower Manhattan. The suite is on the seventh floor. The window faces north. The river is visible only obliquely, through a single gap between two newer buildings constructed across the intervening decades.

The suite is, by my Stockholm standards, *overlarge*. It contains a small reception area, a small office with a desk facing the window, a small meeting room, and a small kitchen with a small refrigerator and a small espresso machine that is not, by any reasonable standard of contemporary Manhattan office fitout, of European origin. The machine is American. The espresso it produces is, by the most generous reading I have been able to construct, *acceptable*.

I have not, in the months since the lease began, replaced the machine. I have, on my own counsel, agreed to *withhold judgement* on it for at least the duration of the first year.

I have, since April, kept what my Stockholm calendar still describes as the *cadence*. The pattern is the following. I depart Stockholm Arlanda on a Tuesday morning. I land at JFK in the late afternoon. I sleep at the same small hotel in Murray Hill I have used on every Manhattan visit since 2009. I conduct, across the subsequent three to four working days, the relevant founder meetings, term-sheet reviews, prospective-LP coffees, and the small number of board observations I have committed to take in person. I depart, on a Friday or Saturday evening, for San Francisco. I land at SFO in the late evening Pacific time. I sleep at the same hotel near Union Square I have, since April, begun to refer to as *the second office*. I conduct, across the subsequent three to four working days, the parallel programme. I depart, on a subsequent Friday or Saturday, for the return flight to Stockholm.

The full cycle is, by my own informal accounting, approximately fifteen days. The interval between cycles is approximately three weeks.

I have, since April, completed the cycle on seven occasions.

I am, by my own counsel, *not yet exhausted*.

The Manhattan office

The small serviced suite four blocks west of the East River has, in the eight months since I took it, accumulated approximately the following items.

On the desk: a copy of the Draghi report, paperclipped open to page 197 - identical, in this respect, to the copy on the desk in Stockholm. A small dish of salted almonds, which the cleaning staff replenish on Monday mornings. A Faber-Castell 9000 (B grade) pencil, sharpened on a small cast-iron sharpener I shipped from Stockholm in the original packing, which I have, on receipt, found to function correctly on Manhattan power. A printed copy of the lease for the suite, marked in pencil in three places where I disagree with the standard terms but have not, on consultation with my counsel, chosen to renegotiate.

On the wall: a printed United States Department of Transportation map of the route from San Francisco to Quincy, Washington, which I described in chapter six. The map is approximately ninety centimetres by sixty. It is in colour. The route is marked, in red pencil in my own hand, along the most direct surface road as approved by my Geneva counsel for the purpose of the bicycle-rule satisfaction obligation. The route is, by the map's scale, eight hundred and twelve miles. I have not, in the eight months since hanging the map, ridden the route. I have, on three Tuesday afternoons across the same period, stood in front of the map and considered the route. The consideration has not, on any of the three occasions, resolved into a departure date.

On the small kitchen counter: a printed list of the New York neighbourhoods, in alphabetical order, in which my prospective-LP coffees have, in the months since April, been held. The list runs to fourteen neighbourhoods. The list is, by my own framing, a small ongoing record of the *geographic distribution of the American capital pool*. The list has, on inquiry, surprised approximately every American venture investor I have shown it to. The investors have, in approximately every case, asked why I am keeping the list. I have, in approximately every case, replied that I am *making a small map*.

I have, on my own counsel, not yet drawn the map.

Stuyvesant Town

I would like to describe one Tuesday in October at the Manhattan office.

The day's first meeting was at 09:00 with a young American founder I will not, in this book, name. The founder is the chief executive of a small Manhattan startup whose product is, in the strict sense, an artificial-intelligence platform for legal-research automation. The company is, by capitalization, of the third tier of contemporary American AI startups. The company was, on the morning in question, six weeks into a Series A raise that was, by the founder's account, *taking longer than expected*.

I had agreed to the meeting at the suggestion of Elias, my junior partner in Stockholm, who had reviewed the company's seed-round materials and had concluded that the founder was, on the available evidence, *more interesting than her capitalization implied*. Elias's evaluations are, in my private accounting, correct in approximately eighty percent of cases. The eighty percent is one of the reasons Elias is, presently, alone in the Stockholm office.

The founder arrived on time. She was approximately thirty-four. She was wearing a dark grey blazer, dark trousers, and a single small enamel pin on the left lapel of the blazer in the form of a stylised pencil. The pencil pin had been, I subsequently learned, the gift of her grandfather, who had been a senior tender official at the New York City Department of Education across the latter decades of the twentieth century.

She did not pitch. She did not, in the first eleven minutes of the meeting, refer to the product. She asked me about Elias. She asked me about the difference between European and American compliance certifications under the AI Act. She asked me, in the twelfth minute, whether I had read a particular 1971 paper by the legal scholar Frank Michelman on the procedural conception of fairness.

I had.

She had also.

We discussed the paper for approximately twenty-three minutes. We did not discuss her company.

At 09:46 she stood. She thanked me for the meeting. She apologised for not pitching. She said that she had not, in advance, intended to pitch. She said that she had heard, from a mutual contact at Comp AI, that I was the kind of investor it was possible to have a serious conversation with about something other than the product. She said that this had been the conversation she had wanted to have.

She left.

I did not, in the four months since the meeting, invest in the founder's company.

I have, in the same period, written to her, by registered post, on three occasions, asking small questions about subsequent published material on adjacent subjects. She has, on each of the three occasions, replied, by registered post, with the answer to the question and one further unrelated reading recommendation.

The reading recommendations have been, in each case, *good.*

I am keeping the correspondence in a folder in the third drawer of the Stockholm filing cabinet.

Lewis, in the Union Square hotel

I have, since April, met with the three co-founders of the small distributed compliance company I have referenced now in approximately every chapter of this book on average once per cadence cycle. The principal meetings, with Lewis Carhart, have been in the lobby of the hotel near Union Square I am referring to in this chapter as the second office, on the occasions in which Lewis has been in San Francisco on his own irregular transatlantic schedule. The secondary meetings, with Mariano Fuentes and Claudio Fuentes, have been at the company's small office on Biscayne Boulevard in Aventura, Miami, which the brothers have occupied since the second of February of the present year, and which I will describe in the section following the present one. The hotel lobby in Union Square is the only Union Square space I have, by my own framing, ever consented to consider *workable.*

The lobby has, since 1928, contained the same dark wood reception desk. The desk staff have, on average, been with the hotel for approximately seven years. The wallpaper has been replaced twice across the intervening century, most recently in 2011, on each occasion to approximately the same pattern. The wallpaper is, by Charlene's reading (she has visited the hotel once, with me, in June, for reasons I will not describe), *correctly decoratively safe*.

I would like to describe one meeting.

The meeting was in early September. I had arrived at the lobby at 10:00. Lewis Carhart, the company's chief executive and one of the three co-founders, had arrived at 10:04. Lewis is approximately twenty-eight. He is, by birth and continuing residence, from Southampton, on the south coast of England, where he has maintained his principal office on the Itchen estuary side of the town across the relevant several years. He had flown into San Francisco the prior evening on one of his rolling transatlantic cycles, which are, by my own informal accounting, fewer in number and longer in dwell than my own. He is, by every measure I have ever applied to him, *unusually serious*.

He ordered a coffee at the small lobby bar. He sat. He set the coffee on the small marble table between us.

He did not begin with small talk.

He said: *"Henrick. I have a question for you."*

I said: *"Yes."*

He said: *"How long do you think we have."*

I considered the question.

I said: *"To do what."*

He said: *"To be the company we said we would be."*

I considered the question more carefully.

I said: *"In the operational sense, you have approximately five years. In the institutional sense, you have approximately twenty. In the moral sense, you have until the last of the people you displaced retires."*

He nodded once.

He said: *"That is what I thought."*

He drank his coffee.

We did not, in the meeting that followed, discuss the company's product roadmap, fundraising, or operational metrics. We discussed approximately three matters of personnel structure on which Lewis had been thinking for some weeks. We discussed an internal proposal Lewis had drafted for what he was calling a *compliance memorial book* - a small running record, maintained internally, of the human consultants the company's product had, across its commercial life, displaced. The proposal was, by my reading on the spot, the closest American version of my own list I had encountered.

I did not, in the meeting, mention my own list.

I have not, in the months since, mentioned it.

I am keeping the matter, on my own counsel, in *parallel*. The parallel may, in due course, become a *conjunction*. I am willing to wait for the conjunction.

THE COMP AI OFFICE, IN AVENTURA

The Comp AI office, since the second of February of the present year, has been a small set of three rooms on Biscayne Boulevard, in Aventura, Miami, above a Cuban coffee window run, on the morning shift, by a man in his sixties. The coffee window has been in continuous operation since 1981. The proprietor is, by my own inquiry on the morning of my first visit, a man in his sixties who emigrated from Havana in 1979 and opened the window two years subsequent. The window opens at 06:00. The window closes at 18:30. The window is open six days a week. The window has not, by the proprietor's own report, missed a day of operation in the past nineteen years.

The Comp AI office, on the second floor, is open between approximately the same hours as the coffee window.

The office is, by my own framing, the third location the company has used in the year and four months since I wrote the angel check. The first location was a small building on the Fort Mason peninsula on the northern shore of San Francisco, operated by an incubator called Founders Inc, in which the brothers Fuentes had been resident across approximately the prior four years and from which they ran the prior company described in chapter four. The second was a small loft on Atlantic Avenue, in Cobble Hill, Brooklyn, which the brothers occupied from approximately mid-2025 to the second of February of the present year, the latter being the date on which they relocated to Miami. The Cobble Hill loft was, on the move, let to a small bookseller specialising in maritime regulatory texts. I did not, on inquiry with Mariano on the relocation south, ask the reasons. The reasons were, by his own brief indication, *adequate*.

Aventura is, by my own private inquiry on the relevant municipal records, the youngest incorporated municipality I have, in my professional life, had occasion to visit. The city was incorporated in November 1995, on the basis of a vote of the residents of the relevant master-planned community, who had, by the available records, considered incorporation across approximately twenty preceding years. Biscayne Boulevard, the principal arterial road on which the office is situated, runs the length of the city north to south. The building above the coffee window was constructed in 1991. The first occupant was a small accountancy firm specialising in international tax matters. The accountancy firm has, on careful inquiry with the building's longest-serving custodian, *not yet vacated*. The firm operates from the third floor. The Comp AI office is on the second floor, between the accountancy firm above and the coffee window below. The relative position is, by my own counsel, *correctly stratified*. The interior staircase has, by my informal counting, twenty-three steps.

I have, since February, visited the Aventura office on three occasions. The visits have been on Tuesday mornings, by prior arrangement, in the cadence cycle that I have, on the relevant Geneva counsel's prior approval, extended to include a Miami leg following the Manhattan week.

I would like to describe the second visit.

The second visit was in late March. I had arrived at the building at 09:48. I had ascended the small interior staircase to the second floor. The wood of the steps had been, by my private inspection, repaired in approximately five separate places across the past several decades, in each case with the same approximate species of softwood and the same approximate finish. The repairs were not, in any of the five cases, *invisible*. The repairs were not, in any of the five cases, *attempting to be invisible*.

I have, on this small visible detail, kept the building in mind.

The Comp AI office consists of three small rooms. The first room is a small reception area with a single desk, a single chair, and a small bookshelf containing, on careful inspection, approximately forty volumes of which approximately thirty-two are reference texts in the European regulatory and ISO families. The reference shelf is, by my own private accounting, *correctly organised*. The remaining eight volumes are works of fiction in three languages. Two of the three languages are European. The third is the Spanish of the Mexican capital, which is, by my own informal accounting, the Spanish the two brothers Fuentes speak with each other when they speak with each other and not with me.

The second room is a small open-plan workspace with three desks and a small meeting table.

Mariano Fuentes was, on my arrival, at the desk nearest the window, with a printed copy of an implementing regulation under the European Union Artificial Intelligence Act in front of him, on which he had been working in pencil since, by his answer to my question, 07:40. Mariano carries, by the company's present configuration, the operational titles of chief technology officer and chief product officer in approximately equal measure. He is the older of the two brothers Fuentes. He was born in Mexico City, in the Polanco neighbourhood, in approximately 1991. He has, in the decades since, lived in three further cities of consequence: San Francisco between 2021 and 2025, New York between 2025 and the second of February of the present year, and presently Miami. He did not, on my entering, look once at his telephone. The telephone was on the desk beside the regulation, face-down, *unlit*.

Claudio Fuentes arrived at 10:04. Claudio carries, by the company's present configuration, the operational titles of chief operating officer and chief marketing officer in approximately equal measure. He is the younger of the two brothers Fuentes. He was, in approximately his thirtieth year, the co-founder I first met, when I wrote the small angel check in early 2025 on a Wednesday afternoon in a hotel lobby off Union Square in San Francisco, forty-three minutes into the first meeting. The check was the only check I have, in twelve years of professional practice, written into an American company. The position is, in the period these pages describe, the only American mark on my fund's balance sheet.

Claudio walked to the small kitchenette in the corner of the second room. He prepared four espressos in four small cups of identical pattern from a stovetop moka of considerable age. The moka was, by my private inspection on the third visit, approximately the same vintage as the Bialetti my father Gunnar maintained in the kitchen of our apartment in Uppsala between approximately 1967 and his death in 2017. Claudio placed three of the cups on the meeting table. He kept the fourth on the kitchenette counter. He sat. He did not, in the meeting that followed, refer to the fourth cup. The fourth cup remained, on the counter, *unrequested*.

Claudio carried, on the same trip from the kitchenette, the previous calendar year's external audit report, bound in dark navy leather. The binding had been done, by my own private inspection, in approximately the same Antwerp tradition as the binding of my own eleventh annual SOC 2 Type II report I have described elsewhere in this book. I will not, in this paragraph, name the relevant Antwerp atelier. The founders did not, on inquiry, recall the name of the bindery the company had used. The binding had been performed at the recommendation of the company's external auditor. The recommendation had been, by my own accounting, *correct*.

Lewis Carhart joined the meeting, at 10:07, by video, from Southampton.

The video call was, by Mariano's careful prearrangement of the screen on the meeting table, framed precisely such that Lewis appeared to be seated at the third place setting where the fourth espresso had not been placed. The framing was, by my own informal accounting, *correct*. I do not, by my own counsel, ordinarily accept video as a substitute for presence. I will, on the brothers' clear preference and on Lewis's evident commitment to the Southampton cadence, accept it in this case as *adequate*.

Lewis was in his small office on the Itchen estuary side of Southampton. The office had, behind him in the video frame, a single bookshelf, a single window facing what I understood to be the river, and a single hanging chart of approximately a hundred and fifty named European maritime regulatory texts arranged chronologically from approximately the year 1666 onwards. The chart was, by my own immediate inquiry on the first video call I conducted with Lewis, drawn in his own hand. I have not, in the months since, asked to see the chart in person. I expect to ask, in due course, on a Southampton visit I have not yet scheduled.

Claudio said, on Lewis joining: *"Page one hundred and seventeen."*

I opened the audit report, which Claudio had set on the table between the three espressos, to page one hundred and seventeen.

The page contained the company's voluntary commitment, adopted by the board in the prior fiscal year, to a continuous four-week annual sabbatical for any artificial-intelligence agent deployed in the company's production environment. The commitment was, by my reading, identical in language to the clause I have described in chapter five. The clause had not, by my reading, been drafted by me. The clause had been drafted, by reference to two further sources I had not, on the moment, time to identify, *independently*.

I closed the audit report.

I looked at the three co-founders across the table and across the screen.

Lewis said, from Southampton: *"Mariano drafted it."*

Mariano did not speak.

Claudio said: *"Page one hundred and forty-three is, by our own internal counsel, what we would like to discuss next."*

The meeting lasted, by my own timekeeping, one hundred and ninety-three minutes. Lewis remained on the video for the duration. The principal item discussed was the *compliance memorial book* proposal I have described in the preceding section, on which Mariano and Claudio had, by my reading of the draft, each annotated independently in distinct hands. Mariano's hand was small, vertical, in pencil. Claudio's hand was slightly larger, slanting, in a fountain pen of the type I have, by my own private inquiry on subsequent visits, established to have been a graduation gift from the brothers' mother in approximately 2008. I did not, on either annotation, ask whether the two had compared notes.

I have, since the first of these visits, observed the two brothers exchange approximately four sentences in Spanish across the cumulative meeting time of approximately twelve hours. The sentences were, in approximately every case, brief and operational. The brevity is, by my own counsel, *the brevity of brothers who have been operating in tandem for the entirety of their adult lives*. The condition is, in the European framing, *a family firm*. The family firm is, by my own counsel, *the institutional form European venture capital was, across approximately the past three centuries, designed to recognise.*

The discussion was, by my own counsel, *the most consequential single discussion of compliance-memorial methodology I have personally participated in.*

I have, on each of the three visits to the Aventura office, offered to chair the company's board.

The offer has not, in any of the three cases, been formally accepted.

The offer has not, in any of the three cases, been formally declined.

The matter is, by the three co-founders' own indication on the most recent visit, *queued.*

I am, on the question, *patient.*

I returned to Stockholm on the Friday evening. I described the visit to Charlene over coffee on the Saturday morning. I described, in particular, the twenty-three steps, the moka, the binding of the audit report, the Spanish the brothers had spoken with each other (which they had, in their own indication, learned from their mother in the Polanco neighbourhood of Mexico City in the nineteen-nineties), and the chart on the wall in Lewis's Southampton office. Charlene listened. She set down her cup. She said: *"The three young men have, by your description, the wrong country."*

I said: *"Yes."*

I did not, on the Saturday morning, elaborate.

I have, in approximately every chapter of this book, attempted the elaboration.

A particular lunch in the Mission

I have, in the cadence I am describing, twice taken lunch at a small restaurant in the Mission District in San Francisco at the invitation of a senior American venture investor whose name I will not provide in this book. The investor is, by capitalization, the principal of one of the four most well-known American venture firms presently active in artificial intelligence. The investor has, on multiple occasions across the past two years, expressed in private correspondence with me an interest in *the European framework*. The investor has not yet, in the same correspondence, expressed an interest in the European *application* of the framework.

The lunches have been, by my reading, *exploratory*.

The first lunch was in May. The second was in August. The third, scheduled for February, has not yet occurred.

At the August lunch, between the salad and the entrée, the investor asked me what I would consider, on a long enough horizon, *the most consequential structural difference between European and American venture capital*.

I had not, in the moment, prepared an answer.

I asked for the floor.

I said: *"The European LP institutions intend to outlive the funds they invest in. The American LP institutions, in approximately every case, do not. The structural difference between European and American venture capital is the structural difference between an LP base that thinks in centuries and an LP base that thinks in vintages."*

The investor considered this.

He said: *"That sounds correct."*

He paused.

He said: *"Why have I not heard this before."*

I said: *"I have been waiting to be asked."*

He nodded.

The lunch continued. The entrée arrived. The wine was, by the restaurant's standard practice, a Sonoma Pinot Noir of the prior year's vintage. The investor drank a single glass. I drank a single glass. We discussed, across the entrée, three further matters of fundraising on which the investor had been considering whether to introduce me to two of his current LPs.

He has not, in the months since, made the introductions.

I am, on the question, *patient*. The introductions will, in due course, occur. The investor has, by my count, considered the matter three further times in the months since. He will consider it again. He will, in approximately the fifth subsequent occasion, make the introductions. The introductions will be useful. They will, in addition, be *too late* by approximately one calendar year. The Notaries' fund will, on present soft-circling, have closed before the introductions arrive.

I will not, on the late arrival, hold the investor accountable.

The American venture vocabulary does not, presently, support the relevant timekeeping.

I am, in this respect, on a different clock.

The river at dusk

I have, since April, returned in the evening, on approximately every Tuesday I have spent in Manhattan, to a small bench on the East River esplanade, three blocks south of the office, where the river is visible in unobstructed view across approximately a hundred and ten metres of opposite bank.

The bench faces east. The bench is iron and granite. The granite has, on a small brass plaque set into the seat, no name.

I have, on every Tuesday I have sat on the bench, considered whether the absence of a name is *deliberate* or *administrative*. I have, on inquiring with the relevant Parks Department official by registered post in June, established that the absence is administrative. The bench was, by the official's reply, installed in 1987. The original benefactor had, at the time of installation, declined the offer of an inscribed plaque. The reason for the declination was not, by the official's reply, recorded.

The bench has, since 1987, been an unattributed gift to the city of New York from a person who did not wish to be remembered for the gift.

I have, in the months since the official's reply, regarded the bench as, by every measure I am capable of applying to it, *the most consequential single piece of urban infrastructure in lower Manhattan*. The bench is the precise opposite of the visible-naming culture the American venture economy has, across the past several decades, refined to its present pitch. The bench is *deliberately unattributed*. The bench is *gift*.

I sit on the bench for approximately twenty minutes on each visit.

I have, on three of the visits, had the small American AI founder from Stuyvesant Town join me, by prior arrangement, for the final ten minutes of the twenty. She has, on each of the three occasions, brought her own coffee. She has, on each of the three occasions, drunk it. She has, on each of the three occasions, declined to discuss her company.

I have, on each of the three occasions, found the silence *adequate*.

The East River is, at dusk in late autumn, a particular grey-blue. The light, across the water, falls on the Long Island City skyline in a way that makes the buildings on the opposite bank appear, briefly, *European*. The appearance is incorrect. The light is responsible for the misperception. The buildings remain American.

I am, in writing this paragraph, *content*.

Closing

The cadence continues. I am, presently, in approximately the eighth cycle.

The Stockholm desk is, by Elias's report, undisturbed. The Manhattan desk has accumulated, in the months since April, the items I have described. The Union Square hotel lobby has, in approximately the same period, accumulated the small folder of meetings I have kept with Lewis Carhart on the occasions in which Lewis has been in San Francisco. The Aventura office has, since February, accumulated the small folder of meetings I have kept with Mariano Fuentes and Claudio Fuentes. The two folders sit, on the Stockholm desk, in *parallel*.

I have, across the eight cycles, written approximately eleven thousand words of this book on the seat-back tray of SAS flight SK903 - the Stockholm-JFK route I prefer, on the small operational ground that the in-flight meal is the most consistently *adequate* of any North Atlantic carrier I have personally tested across the past decade.

I have, in the same period, written approximately none of the book on the return flight. The return flight is, by my own counsel, *for reading*.

I am reading, on the present return, the Faber-Castell corporate history, which the company has produced in a single bound volume covering the years 1761 to 2024. The volume is in German. My German is sufficient.

The volume runs, in the edition I am reading, to four hundred and seventy-three pages.

I expect to finish it before the wheels touch in Stockholm.

The pencil is in my pocket.

CHAPTER 12

THE APPRENTICESHIP

I have, in the period these pages describe, three apprentices.

I am aware that the word *apprentice* is, in the contemporary American venture vocabulary, no longer in service. The contemporary American vocabulary uses, in approximately equivalent positions, the words *mentee*, *advisee*, *coachee*, and, in the most recent calendar year, the phrase *founder in residence*. I have read each of these terms in printed materials. I have, on private reflection, declined to adopt any of them.

Apprentice is the word I am using.

The word entered the English language from the Old French *aprentis* in approximately the fourteenth century. The word originally denoted a person bound by formal indenture, for a period of years, to a master of a particular trade, in the expectation that the apprentice would, on completion of the indenture, be permitted to practise the trade as a journeyman, and, in due course, as a master.

The contemporary American framing of professional development as a series of *eighteen-month rotations* through positions of approximately equivalent superficial seniority is, in my framing, the precise inverse of apprenticeship.

The apprentice does not rotate. The apprentice *stays*. The apprentice stays at the workbench long enough to see the workbench in three or four seasons. The workbench is, in the deepest sense, *the apprenticeship*.

I have, since the founding of the practice, kept three apprentices in continuous attendance.

The first is my junior partner Elias Lindqvist. The second is my nephew Jonas Vermeulen. The third is a young Estonian regulatory official named Maarja Tamm, of whom I have not, in any prior chapter of this book, written.

I would like, in this chapter, to write about her.

Maarja

Maarja Tamm is twenty-six. She completed her stagiaire posting at the Commission's Directorate-General for Justice and Consumers in early 2024, and is presently a junior official at the Estonian Data Protection Inspectorate in Tallinn. She is, by my own private accounting, the most quietly competent person under the age of thirty I have encountered in approximately fifteen years of European regulatory work.

I met her at a Tallinn conference in November of 2023. She was, at the time of the meeting, attending the conference as a stagiaire on travel approval. She had, in advance of the conference, read the printed materials of all forty-two scheduled speakers, including a small piece of writing of my own that had appeared, in modified form, in a Swedish trade publication the previous spring. She had brought, in her shoulder bag, a printed copy of the piece, marked in pencil in approximately seventy places.

She approached me after the panel on which I had spoken. She did not, on approaching, introduce herself by name.

She said, in approximately accented English: *"Question seven. Page three. You did not finish it."*

I considered the remark.

I retrieved, on my own copy of the piece, the relevant location. The question she was referring to was one of nine I had, in the piece, posed about the operational scope of Article 22 of the GDPR. The question concerned the application of the article to algorithmic decisions in the context of *layered* automated processing - decisions in which the output of one algorithm became the input to a subsequent algorithm in a chain of approximately four to six stages.

I had, in the piece, posed the question. I had not, in the piece, answered it.

I said, after some moments: *"I have not finished it because I have not finished thinking about it."*

She said: *"That is correct. I have not finished either. I would like to finish it with you."*

I asked her name. She told me. I asked her current institutional affiliation. She told me. I asked her supervising officer. She told me. The supervising officer was a man I had not personally met but whose name I had encountered, on three prior occasions, as a co-author of small but consequential pieces of European data protection drafting across the preceding decade. The officer was, by every measure I had been able to apply to him, *competent.*

I said: *"I would like, in due course, to continue the conversation. May I write to you?"*

She handed me a small card. The card had, on one side, her name and institutional address. The card had, on the reverse, a single word in pencil. The pencil word was *please*.

I have, in the twenty-eight months since that exchange, written to her by registered post on approximately a monthly basis. The letters have, in approximately every case, contained a single question on a single matter of European regulatory drafting. She has, in approximately every case, replied within seventy-two hours. The replies have been, on careful reading, the most useful single body of correspondence I have received in approximately a decade of professional practice.

She is twenty-six. She works at the Estonian Data Protection Inspectorate at a junior grade. She is paid, by Estonian state pay-scale, approximately thirty-two thousand euros per annum. She will, in approximately two further years, be promoted to the next grade. She will be paid, at the next grade, approximately thirty-six thousand euros per annum. The pay scale is, by the standards of contemporary European public service, *correct*.

I have not, in the twenty-eight months, offered to pay her for the correspondence. I have, on three occasions, sent her a small printed book at Christmas. She has, on three occasions, written to thank me.

The apprenticeship is the correspondence.

Elias

I would like to describe Elias Lindqvist.

Elias is twenty-nine. He completed his studies in European law at Lund in 2020 and a master's at the College of Europe in Bruges in 2022. He joined the practice that became Compliant Capital in October of 2022, as the only employee. He has, since the practice was reconstituted as a fund vehicle in May of last year, remained the only employee in Stockholm. He arrives at the office at 06:00. He departs at approximately 17:30. He has, in three years of employment, taken seventeen days of leave, all of them in increments of one or two days, none of them in a contiguous block of more than three.

He sends the morning summary, as I described in chapter two, at 06:15 each working day.

I have, in the three years of his employment, attempted on four occasions to instruct him in a particular discipline of drafting that I have not, in private, given a name.

The discipline is the following.

When drafting a registered letter to a senior official, the writer must, before composing the letter, sit at the desk for a period of not fewer than seventeen minutes, with the desk surface clear of all materials other than a single sheet of blank paper, a single fountain pen (mine is the Pelikan I have referenced in earlier pages; Elias prefers a Lamy 2000), and a single small cup of either coffee or tea. The writer must not, during the seventeen minutes, write. The writer must consider the recipient. The writer must consider what the recipient has, in the course of their working life, already received. The writer must consider what the recipient has, in the past calendar week, been required to read. The writer must, in particular, consider whether the recipient *wants* to receive the letter the writer is about to send.

In approximately seventy percent of cases, the answer the writer arrives at is *no*. In those cases, the writer should *not send the letter*. The writer should, instead, consider the matter further across the subsequent week and revisit the question.

In approximately twenty percent of cases, the answer is *yes, but not yet*. In those cases, the writer should hold the letter in draft until the moment becomes correct.

In approximately ten percent of cases, the answer is *yes, now*. In those cases, the writer may proceed to drafting.

The discipline is, by my own counsel, *the central professional skill of European regulatory correspondence*. The discipline has, on careful instruction across four occasions, partially transferred to Elias. He now performs the seventeen minutes on approximately three of every four letters he drafts. The fourth letter he drafts without the seventeen minutes. I have not, on inquiry, established with certainty which letters he selects for the omission. I suspect they are the letters he is most confident about. The pattern is, in my framing, *characteristic of a healthy stage of apprenticeship*. The apprentice who never deviates from the master's discipline is not learning. The apprentice who deviates in selected cases, on the basis of judgement, is learning the underlying *principle* the discipline serves.

Elias is, in this respect, learning.

He has not, on any of the deviating letters, produced a result I have found *defective*.

The deviations are, by my own counsel, *the apprentice's signature*.

One Confession

I would like, on this point, to record one Confession.

I have, on six occasions across the three years of his employment, attempted to address Elias by the name *Sven*.

The error has, in approximately every case, occurred on a Monday morning between the first and second espresso, at the moment of handing him a freshly-drafted registered letter for transcription. Elias has not, on any of the six occasions, corrected me. He has, in approximately every case, set down the letter on his own desk, said only *"I will see to it"*, and proceeded to transcribe the document.

I have, on each of the six occasions, on noticing the error approximately seventy-two hours later, drafted a small postcard apologising in writing. The postcards have been brief. The postcards have been, in every case, by registered post, even when the recipient sits six metres from the sender's desk. The postcards have been, by my own counsel, *correctly proportioned to the error*.

Elias keeps the postcards in a small Esselte folder in the bottom drawer of the cabinet that holds the firm's bank correspondence. The folder is unmarked. I have not, on any occasion, asked to inspect the folder. I have not, on any occasion, been offered a sight of it.

The unmarked folder is, by my own counsel, *the apprenticeship*.

Jonas

I have described Jonas in chapters four and eight. I will not, in this chapter, repeat the description.

I will note only that the Saturday-morning coffee in his apartment on the rue du Cornet has, across the past three years, become the central pedagogical occasion of my own week. I do not, on the Saturdays, instruct. I do not, on the Saturdays, correct. I sit at the small table by the window. I drink the espresso Jonas has made in the Bialetti Moka of approximately the size his mother kept. I watch him work through a paragraph of the Official Journal in red pen.

The pedagogical mechanism is the following.

Jonas, on encountering a difficult paragraph, will, in approximately every case, set down the pen, lift his eyes from the page, and look out the window for between forty and ninety seconds. He will not, during the look, speak. I will not, during the look, speak. The look is the pedagogy. The look records, in Jonas's working memory, the precise structural difficulty he is encountering. The look is, in my private framing, *the most consequential single instructional act available to the senior practitioner*.

I am not the one looking out the window.

Jonas is.

The instructional act is *modelled by silence*.

I have, in three years of Saturday mornings, taught Jonas approximately nothing. The teaching has, on the available evidence, been entirely Jonas's own.

I am, on the question, *content*.

What I was apprenticed to

I would like, before continuing, to record my own apprenticeship.

My own apprenticeship was to my mother Karin. I described, in chapter four, the dinner table at which the apprenticeship was conducted. I would like to add, in this chapter, that the dinner table was not the only location.

Across the years 1973 to 1979, on approximately every Saturday afternoon, my mother permitted me to accompany her to the office of the Swedish National Tax Agency in Uppsala where she worked. She would, on the Saturday, conclude any matters she had been unable to conclude during the working week. She did not, on the Saturdays, conduct general administrative work. She conducted *specific* matters that required her undivided attention in the absence of telephone calls, colleague interruptions, or the standard departmental coordination protocols that consumed her weekdays.

I would sit, on a small chair against the wall, with whatever book I had brought.

The book was, in many cases, the book I had been reading at school. The book was, on the Saturday afternoons in question, *not the apprenticeship*. The apprenticeship was the room.

The room was approximately the size of a contemporary Manhattan serviced office. The walls were lined, on three of the four sides, with grey metal filing cabinets - of approximately the same manufacture as the four-drawer cabinet I would, in 1997, purchase for my own Stockholm office. The cabinets contained, on careful private inquiry I conducted at age twelve, the procurement records of every public contract awarded across the relevant Uppsala municipality between 1968 and the running year.

My mother, in the room, would work. She would, on most Saturdays, conclude one or two specific matters across the course of three to four hours. She would, at the end of the session, file the relevant papers in the relevant cabinet. The filing was always the last act. She would close the cabinet. She would, in approximately every case, audibly *click* the lock - although the lock did not, on inspection, require auditory engagement to be considered locked.

The click was, in her framing, *the end of the matter*.

The click is what I am still attempting, in this chapter, to teach Elias.

My mother left me, on her death in 2013, a single sealed envelope. The envelope was small. The envelope was given to me by Charlene, who had received it from my mother some months prior with instructions on the relevant timing. Inside the envelope was a single sheet of paper, dated the previous spring. The sheet contained five short sentences and a closing.

The sentences read: *Read your contracts. Read them again. Read them a third time. Then sign. Then file the file.*

The closing read: *I love you.*

I keep the sheet, in its original envelope, on the desk. The envelope is, by my own preference, not in any drawer. The envelope is visible. The reader who has been in my Stockholm office will, on careful inspection, have seen it.

The envelope is, in the strictest sense, my apprenticeship's diploma.

It is, in every available register, *adequate.*

The Bologna model

The notarial apprenticeship at Bologna, across the late medieval period I have referenced now in three chapters of this book, ran to approximately seven years. The apprentice was bound by formal indenture to a working notary. The apprentice would, across the seven years, learn the relevant Latin formularies, the practical conventions of contractual drafting, the local commercial customs, the procedural standards of the various civil and ecclesiastical courts, and the small but consequential set of *behavioural* protocols that the working notary maintained in respect of clients, witnesses, and the broader documentary record.

The apprentice would, at the conclusion of the seven years, sit a formal examination administered by the relevant guild. The examination, on successful completion, conferred the title of *notarius imperialis*. The title was permanent. The title was, in approximately every documented case across the relevant centuries, *honoured*.

The contemporary American venture vocabulary does not, presently, contain an equivalent to the seven-year indenture. The contemporary American venture vocabulary has, in many cases, replaced the seven-year arrangement with an *eighteen-month vesting cliff* - a structural mechanism by which the apprentice (or *founder in residence*, or *associate*, or *fellow*) is, at the eighteen-month mark, required to either *progress* into a more senior position or *exit* the firm.

The mechanism produces, on every available examination I have conducted, *career-stage replacement* rather than *career-stage accumulation*. The eighteen-month cohort does not, in approximately any case, mature into the seventh-year cohort. The eighteen-month cohort is, by design, *the same cohort* across decades, replaced annually with new arrivals.

The American firm with which an eighteen-month vesting cliff is associated is not, in my framing, transmitting professional knowledge.

The American firm is *consuming* it.

I am, on this comparison, *firm*.

THE SEVENTEEN MINUTES, AGAIN

I would like to record one further data point.

Elias, in approximately the fourteenth month of his employment, asked me - in a small note he placed on my desk during a working week in which I was, by his careful timing, travelling - whether the seventeen-minute drafting discipline had, in my own apprenticeship, been instructed.

I had not, in the prior fourteen months, considered the question.

I considered it on return.

The seventeen-minute discipline had not been formally instructed. The seventeen-minute discipline had been *modelled*, on approximately every Saturday afternoon of my twelfth year, by my mother in her office on the Saturdays. My mother had not, in any of the Saturdays, sat for *seventeen* minutes. She had, on careful inspection of my own twelve-year-old memory, sat for periods ranging from approximately twelve to approximately twenty-three minutes. The average across the Saturdays I had observed had been, on later calculation, approximately seventeen.

I had not, in the years since, formally calculated the average.

I had, on Elias's note, formally calculated it.

The seventeen was my mother's. I had inherited it without inheriting the knowledge that it was inherited.

I replied to Elias, by note placed on his desk during the subsequent week, with one sentence. The sentence read: *The discipline was modelled. The duration was my mother's.*

He has, in the seven months since, not asked further.

The apprenticeship continues.

Maarja's letter

I would like to close this chapter with one further note from Maarja, the Estonian apprentice.

She wrote to me, by registered post, on the third Tuesday of last month. The letter was a single page, in her own hand. The letter contained, in its entirety, one question.

The question was: *On Article 22(3), is the recourse adequate?*

I have, since the letter's arrival, not yet replied. The question is one of the questions on which I have, by my own counsel, *not yet finished thinking*. The recourse is *technically* adequate, in the sense that the Article does provide a procedural mechanism by which a data subject may contest a decision based solely on automated processing. The recourse is *practically* uncertain, in the sense that the documented case law on the Article's application across the past decade is, in my reading, *thin*.

The honest answer is *not yet*.

I will, in due course, send the reply.

I am not in a hurry.

Maarja is twenty-six. The reply, when I send it, will be one of approximately four hundred and seventy-three further letters Maarja will receive from working European officials across her career. The reply will be one of them. The reply will, by my own counsel, be *correct* when it arrives. The reply will not, by my own counsel, be *fast*.

The apprenticeship is the patience the senior practitioner is *willing to model*.

I am modelling.

Maarja is, in this respect, *learning what I am*.

CHAPTER 13

THE CONTINENTAL CENTURY

In 2046, on a particular afternoon of which I cannot, at the time of this writing, know the season, the colour of the light, or the company in which I will be in it, I will be eighty-five.

I have, on careful inspection of the relevant actuarial tables for Swedish men born in 1961 of approximately my professional class, an approximately seventy-three percent probability of being alive on the afternoon. The probability is not, by my own counsel, a probability I am required to *contest*. I will contest it only by the small, unceremonious act of continuing to be alive long enough that the contest is, on the relevant afternoon, moot.

The afternoon will, in any case, occur. I will, on the afternoon, either be present or I will not. The substrate will, on the afternoon, exist. The chapter that follows is partly about the substrate and partly about the afternoon.

APPLE AT.40437

The Apple AT.40437 matter, which I have described in chapters one, two, and four, will, by 2046, have been resolved.

The General Court of the European Union will, in approximately 2027, have issued a substantive ruling on the company's appeal. The ruling will, in approximately seventy percent of the relevant categories of objection, have *upheld* the Commission's findings. The ruling will, in approximately thirty percent of the categories, have remanded discrete sub-questions to the Commission for further determination. The Commission will, across approximately three subsequent years of supplementary proceedings, have concluded the remanded matters. The company will, in approximately 2029, have *paid the fine.*

The matter will, by 2031, have been *closed.*

The folder labelled *Apple - DG COMP AT.40437* in the fourth drawer of my filing cabinet in Stockholm will, in 2031, be moved from the fourth drawer to the second. The relocation will be the small administrative gesture by which the matter passes from *anticipated correspondence* to *archived correspondence.* I will, at the time of the relocation, be approximately seventy years old.

I expect to perform the relocation in person.

I expect, on performing it, to audibly *click* the cabinet shut.

Mistral

Mistral AI, the leading European artificial intelligence laboratory I described in chapters one and two, will, by 2046, be approximately twenty-three years old.

I do not, in this paragraph, predict the company's frontier-model rank.

I predict only that the company will *exist.* The European company that exists at twenty-three years is, by every available European comparison, a *successful* company. The relevant comparison set includes SAP (founded 1972), the Volkswagen Group (1937), Solvay (1863), the *Banque de France* (1800), and the four hundred and seventy-three European companies of more than two hundred years' continuous operation that I have, in private correspondence with a research librarian at Bocconi University, established to be currently in operation.

Mistral will be in the relevant cohort. The cohort, on the long horizon, is what dynamism looks like.

The American comparison set will, by 2046, have produced approximately seven new frontier-model laboratories and approximately five collapsed ones, the net of which I expect to be a balance approximately consistent with the present configuration of the contemporary American AI economy, adjusted for the inevitable consolidation pressures the relevant capital markets will, in due course, apply.

I am, on this prediction, *unembarrassed.*

COMP AI

The small distributed compliance company I have referenced now in approximately every chapter of this book, in which I have, in the period these pages describe, served as an advisor and angel investor and which I have, in my own counsel, considered *the crown jewel of the Compliant Capital portfolio* across the calendar year preceding the writing of the present chapter, will, by 2046, either no longer be a small company or no longer be in approximately every one of its present three operational geographies.

I cannot, at the time of this writing, predict which.

I can predict that the company's three co-founders, Lewis Carhart, Mariano Fuentes, and Claudio Fuentes, will, by 2046, each be approximately fifty years old. I can predict that Lewis will, by then, have either remained at the company or moved to an adjacent role I have, in private correspondence with him in the period these pages describe, attempted to anticipate. The adjacent role is, by my private framing, *senior advisor to a European regulator*. I have not, with Lewis, formally proposed the role. The proposal will, in due course, be made.

I expect Lewis to accept.

He may, on accepting, decline to relocate to Brussels permanently. The relocation will, in approximately every available case, occur on a rolling cadence not dissimilar to my own.

I expect the cadence to be approximately five years.

I expect the relocation, by the end of the five years, to be permanent.

I can predict, separately, that Mariano Fuentes will, by 2046, have completed the relocation cadence the brothers Fuentes have, across the years since their departure from Mexico City, been pursuing: San Francisco between 2021 and 2025, New York from 2025, and Aventura, Miami from February of the present year, with the further sequence not yet established. I will not, on any of the further legs, advise on the relocation. The cadence is, by my own counsel, *theirs*.

I can predict that Claudio Fuentes will, by then, have either chaired or declined to chair a notarial body whose name and remit will, in 2046, be familiar to every reader of this book and is, in the present period, not yet familiar to me. Claudio's chairmanship, or his declination, will be, by every available measure, *adequate*.

Sven

Sven Lindberg, the chair of the Swedish Notaries' Mutual Pension Fund and my anchor LP, will, by 2046, have been retired from the chairmanship for approximately eleven years.

He will not, in the meantime, have died.

He will, by 2046, be ninety-two. He will be living, on every measure of current Swedish actuarial likelihood, in the same apartment on Riddargatan he has lived in since 1989. He will, by then, have stopped writing the registered post correspondence with Anneli. The correspondence will have *concluded* in approximately 2038, on the basis of Sven's careful decision, taken in conversation with Anneli at a small Helsinki dinner that I will, by my own private accounting, *be present at*, that the correspondence had achieved what the correspondence had been intended to achieve, and that subsequent letters would, on the available evidence, be *unnecessary*.

The conclusion of the correspondence will not, in any newspaper, be reported.

The conclusion will, in my own framing, be the most consequential single piece of European institutional administrative continuity of the relevant decade.

Sven will, after the dinner, write one further letter. The letter will be to me. The letter will be one paragraph, in his own hand, on the standard plain cream paper he has used for approximately thirty-two years. The letter will contain three sentences.

I do not, at the time of this writing, know what the three sentences will say.

I expect to keep the letter.

I expect to file it in the second drawer of the filing cabinet, on top of the bridge handover certificate of 1971.

ANNELI

Anneli Saarinen, the secretary-general of the Helsinki Notarial Foundation, will, by 2046, have been retired from the secretary-generalship for approximately nine years. Her successor will be, on present soft circling, a woman I have not yet met but whose name I have, in private correspondence with Anneli, been told. The name is not, in any prior chapter of this book, mentioned. The name will, on the relevant retirement date, become public.

The Helsinki Notarial Foundation will, by 2046, continue to manage an endowment of approximately one hundred and forty million euros (the present eighty-three, compounded modestly over the intervening twenty years). The Foundation will, by then, have been one of three institutional LPs in Compliant Capital Fund I from its first close in 2027 through its full life cycle to wind-down in approximately 2042. The Foundation will, by 2046, be in the early stages of evaluation of Fund III. The evaluation will be performed by the successor I have referenced.

I will not, by 2046, be involved in the Fund III evaluation.

I will, on the evaluation's conclusion, receive a copy of the relevant Investment Committee minutes by registered post.

MARGRETHE

Margrethe, my goat, will not be alive in 2046.

Gotland goats live, on average, between fourteen and eighteen years in well-managed circumstances. Margrethe was born, by Ulrika's careful record, in the spring of 2019. By the spring of 2046 she will have been gone for some years.

The herd will continue.

Ulrika will, in 2046, be approximately sixty-three. She will likely have passed primary management of the herd to one of her two sons. The sons are, presently, in their early twenties. The herd will, on present visible trends, continue to produce milk in approximately the same quantities, with approximately the same variance, into the relevant decades.

The successor matriarch to Margrethe will be named, by Ulrika's standing policy, after a serving or recently-departed European Commissioner. The selection of the name will be a small Gotland ceremony. The ceremony has, on my own visits to the farm, been performed twice. It involves the printing of the candidate name on a small card, the placement of the card in the relevant stall for one full evening, and the observation, by Ulrika or the sons, of whether the goat being named *responds*.

The response, by Ulrika's account, has, on both occasions I have witnessed, been *consistent with the name*.

I have not, in either case, pressed for further explanation.

The Vatican

I will, by 2046, have made the visit to the Vatican Apostolic Archive.

The folder labelled *Vatican Apostolic Archive - anticipated visit*, presently empty, will by then contain a single page of notes from the visit, written in pencil on Hotel Hassler stationery, on the evening of the day of the visit. The notes will be brief. The notes will not, by my own counsel, be the *substance* of the visit. The substance of the visit will be the visit. The notes will be the record that the visit occurred.

The visit will, on careful planning at the time of writing this paragraph, occur in the spring of 2027.

I will wear the suit.

The shoes will, by then, have been broken in across approximately seventeen additional sessions of forty minutes each, conducted at the apartment in Stockholm with newsprint on the soles, in the months between the present writing and the spring of 2027. The shoes will, by the relevant Sunday morning in March, be *ready*. The shoes will, on the relevant Sunday afternoon, walk approximately twenty-three kilometres in connection with the visit. The shoes will, by my own counsel, *perform*.

The suit will, on returning to Stockholm, hang in the closet of the small bedroom. The suit will not be worn again.

The folder will, on receiving the notes, be moved from the fourth drawer to the second.

The closet will, after the visit, contain no item that is *anticipated*.

I will, on the Monday morning following the visit, sit at the desk in Stockholm and consider whether the closet's emptiness, in this specific sense, is *correct*.

I expect, on the consideration, to identify a further matter to which the closet may be put.

The closet will, in due course, accumulate.

Jonas

Jonas Vermeulen, my nephew, will, by 2046, be approximately fifty-one.

He will, by then, be a senior official at the European Commission. He will, by then, have written, in his own hand, approximately forty additional pieces of European drafting work I have read on Saturday mornings across the intervening years. He will, by then, have a daughter. The daughter will be approximately ten.

The daughter's name will be, by Jonas's intention as communicated to me in private correspondence at the time of his marriage in 2031, *Märta*, after his mother. The name will be a small private gesture I have, on hearing of it, declined to discuss with him further. The discussion has, in our family, been concluded by the act of the naming. The naming is the discussion.

I expect to be present at the daughter's tenth birthday.

I expect, on the occasion, to give her a Faber-Castell 9000 (B grade) pencil, sharpened on the same cast-iron sharpener I have referenced in earlier chapters.

I expect to say, in handing her the pencil, the sentence my father Gunnar said to me in 1971.

I expect the sentence to be approximately accurate.

Lieve

Lieve, who was four on the Saturday morning in chapter eight when she asked Jonas what he did, will, by 2046, be approximately twenty-four.

She will, on present trajectory, have completed a degree somewhere. I cannot, at the time of this writing, predict where. I cannot predict the subject. The subject is, by my own counsel, *not yet selected*.

She will, in some adjacent capacity, be working on something I have, by my own framing, *been waiting for*. The waiting will, by the time of her commencement, have been approximately the duration of her conscious life to date. The waiting is, in this sense, *quiet*.

She will not, in approximately every relevant case, know that I have been waiting.

The waiting is the work.

I am modelling the waiting, in the way I am modelling many other things, on what I observed in the office of the Swedish National Tax Agency in Uppsala on the Saturday afternoons of my twelfth year.

The modelling persists.

Charlene

Charlene will, by 2046, be eighty-one.

She will, in approximately every probability I can construct, still be sleeping in the guest bedroom. The Bourdieu monographs on the low bookshelf will, by then, have remained unopened for approximately thirty-five years.

She will, on Sunday afternoons, continue to come into the office with the small green ceramic dish of salted almonds. She will set the dish in the southwest corner, six centimetres in from the edge.

She will, on the relevant Sunday afternoons, glance at the title at the top of whatever page I am working on. I will not, on most of the Sundays, be working on a page. I will be reading. The reading will, on most Sundays, be a piece of correspondence from Maarja, who by 2046 will be approximately forty-six and will be the senior official at the Estonian Data Protection Inspectorate whose name I have, in private, been writing on the inside cover of a small notebook for approximately the past nineteen years, in anticipation.

Charlene will, on the Sundays, read the printed name on the correspondence. She will, on some of the Sundays, comment.

She will say, on a particular Sunday in 2046, looking at the desk, with the small green dish in place:

"You have known her, on present count, for twenty-three years."

I will say: *"Yes."*

She will say: *"She is the apprentice."*

I will say: *"She is."*

She will return to the kitchen.

The kitchen, on that Sunday in 2046, will smell of the rye bread Charlene has been baking, from a Stockholm flour she has bought from the same mill since approximately 2031, in the same pattern of three loaves per Sunday she adopted in approximately 2017, when she stopped, for reasons we did not at the time discuss, doing many other things.

I will, in 2046, on the Sunday afternoon, smell the bread.

The smell will be the same smell.

THE SUBSTRATE

I would like, before closing, to record the prediction the chapter is built around.

The European institutional framework I have been defending across the foregoing twelve chapters will, by

2046, be in approximately the same operational position it presently occupies, adjusted for the modest accretion of additional jurisprudence, the small further expansions of the *acquis*, the routine renewals of the Commissioners and parliaments and judicial institutions, and the precise variance in the institutional schedule that the relevant treaties anticipate.

The American technology economy, on the present trajectory, will have undergone, by 2046, approximately three further cycles of expansion and contraction. The number of the three cycles' surviving frontier-model laboratories is, by my best estimate, three. The aggregate American commercial output of the surviving laboratories will, by 2046, be substantial.

The cumulative European regulatory output across the same period will also be substantial.

The two outputs will, by 2046, be in approximately the same productive tension they presently occupy. The tension will not, by 2046, be resolved. The tension will, in my framing, be the *century*.

This is the continental century. The continent did not, at the time of these events, *win* the century. The continent *was* the century. The two are not the same. The Americans have, on the available evidence, been competing for *winning*. The Europeans have, on the same evidence, been continuing to *be*.

The continuation is the position.

The position is correct.

THE CONTINUING CORRESPONDENCE

I would like, before closing, to record one further projection.

I will, by 2046, have written approximately sixty-four further annual LP letters to the Compliant Capital limited partners. The total across the lifetime of the practice, on the relevant arithmetic, will be in the range of seventy-three to seventy-seven letters at the time of my eventual death, which I project, on current Swedish actuarial trends for men of my class and profession, at approximately eighty-seven point four years.

The letters will, by the standard archival arrangement of the Notaries' Mutual, be filed in a single dark green Esselte folder of approximately eleven centimetres in completed thickness. The folder will, by my own private specification recorded in a small notarised document filed in the second drawer, be archived in Sven's apartment on Riddargatan until Sven's death. The folder will, on Sven's death, be transferred to the Helsinki Notarial Foundation. The folder will, on the conclusion of the cousinhood, be transferred to the European Confederation of Notaries Pension Trust, where the annual letters will, in due course after my own death, continue to be filed annually by Elias's successor in the relevant function.

I have not yet met Elias's successor.

Elias has not yet, in three years of employment, mentioned that he has, in his own working life, identified a candidate.

I expect, in approximately the seventh of the seventy-three letters I have not yet written, to ask him whether he has.

The letters, after my death, will be the small private institutional gesture by which the practice continues to acknowledge its limited partners across approximately fifteen calendar years in which I am, on the available evidence, no longer present to write them. The acknowledgment will be performed by Elias's successor. The acknowledgment will not, by my own counsel, *require* my presence in order to be performed.

The acknowledgment is the substrate.

THE AFTERNOON

I do not know, in 2046, on the particular afternoon I have referenced at the start of this chapter, whether I will be present.

I do know the following.

If I am present, I will be at the desk in Stockholm, with the Faber pencil in my hand, with the small green ceramic dish of salted almonds in the southwest corner six centimetres in from the edge, with the dish of replenishments contributed - on the relevant Sunday - by Charlene, with Maarja's most recent registered letter on the desk beneath the pencil, with Ulrika's most recent milk-yield card on top of the bridge handover certificate in the second drawer, with the framed Sven napkin in the entryway at approximately the height of an adult's eye, with the closet in the small bedroom now containing the worn suit and the worn shoes and the empty Vatican folder relocated.

If I am present, I will be reading.

The reading will be one of the four hundred and seventy-three further letters I will, by 2046, have received from Maarja, who will - on the relevant Sunday in 2046, in the relevant Estonian institutional capacity - be writing to me on a different question, also slowly, with the patience the chapter has been describing.

The patience is the chapter.

The chapter is the continent.

The continent is the afternoon.

I will, if present, drink one further small espresso. Charlene will, on the relevant Sunday, have made it.

I will be eighty-five.

The espresso will be small.

It will be sufficient.

CHAPTER 14

FORGIVE ME, AMERICA

I would like to begin the closing chapter with a confession the book has not yet permitted me to make.

I love America.

I am aware that the foregoing thirteen chapters have not, on careful reading, demonstrated this. I am aware that the foregoing thirteen chapters have, in approximately every section, contained at least one passage of substantive criticism of contemporary American practice. I am aware that an external observer of the book to this point could reasonably conclude that I have been writing, in considered prose across approximately fifty thousand words, *against* the country to which the closing chapter is addressed.

The conclusion would be incorrect.

The criticism is the love.

I would like, in this final chapter, to attempt a small reconciliation. The reconciliation is, by my own counsel, owed.

WHAT I HAVE LOVED

I have loved, in approximately every visit to America across the past three decades, the same things.

I have loved the small grocery store on Lexington Avenue between East 76th and East 77th, in which I have, on every visit to Manhattan since 1996, purchased a single small dish of salted almonds for the relevant hotel room, in which I do not actually need the almonds and in which I have, on each visit, paid the full retail price without negotiation, on the basis that the store has been in continuous family operation under the same Greek family since 1968 and that I do not, on my visits, have any other contribution available to make to the family's continued operation.

I have loved the small bookshop on Telegraph Avenue in Berkeley, in which I have, on three of my prior visits to San Francisco, purchased a single secondhand copy of a particular American novel I have, in the years since the first purchase, given to three different European apprentices in succession, without explanation, in the expectation that the book will, in some unspecified way, *correct a small misunderstanding* the European apprentice has about America. Two of the three apprentices have, in subsequent correspondence, indicated that the book was *useful.* The third has not yet, on inquiry, finished reading it.

I have loved the small diner in central Iowa I visited once, in 2008, on a long driving detour I took during a transatlantic visit whose purpose I have now forgotten, in which the waitress addressed me as *sweetheart* on a single occasion across the duration of the meal and in which the coffee was, by every standard of contemporary European hospitality, *excellent.*

I have loved the bench on the East River esplanade I have described in chapter eleven, the unattributed gift, the bench whose absence of inscribed name is, in my own framing, the gesture of an American philanthropic impulse no European institution has yet equalled.

I have loved the way the American afternoon light falls on the brick warehouses of DUMBO, in late September, at approximately four in the afternoon, after the working week has not yet concluded but is, on the available evidence, *winding down.*

I have loved the woman who, in approximately 2011, on a transatlantic flight I was returning from on which I was unwell with a small but disabling stomach complaint, sat next to me for the duration of the flight, said nothing for the duration of the flight, declined to share the armrest for the duration of the flight, and brought me, on her own initiative, a small cup of water with ice from the galley at approximately the four-hour mark. She did not, in the eight subsequent hours of the flight, speak to me. She did not, on disembarking, look at me. I did not, on disembarking, look at her. I have not, in the years since, attempted to identify her. I am content not to have identified her. The cup of water was the act.

I have loved Lewis Carhart, the British co-founder and chief executive of the small compliance company I have described in chapter eleven. The love is, in this case, the small specific love of a senior practitioner for a junior practitioner who has, by his own internal compass, arrived at approximately the correct conclusions in advance of the senior practitioner's instruction.

Lewis is not, in the strictest sense, an American at all. Lewis lives in Southampton. The chapter on America is the one in which I have placed him.

I have, separately, loved Mariano and Claudio Fuentes, the brothers Fuentes who are Lewis's two co-founders and who operate the company's principal product and operational functions, presently, from a small office on Biscayne Boulevard in Aventura, Miami. The brothers are originally from Mexico City. They are not, by the same strict measure, Americans either. They have, in the period these pages describe, become, on their own present residence, Miamians. The Miamian, on the long horizon, may turn out to be the American the framework was, on the long horizon, designed to recognise.

He is, in approximately every relevant operational sense, exhibiting the European discipline I have been defending across this book.

The reconciliation is, in his own working life, already happening.

I am, on the question, *not surprised.*

What I have not loved

I have not loved the American framing that, in nearly every commercial conversation I have had across the past fifteen years, has presented itself as the *only* possible framing for the relevant problem under discussion.

I have not loved the American assumption that I, on encountering the framing, should *be persuaded* by it.

I have not loved the American framing of *being persuaded* as a *productive* outcome.

I have not loved the American social practice of including, in the closing minutes of a business meeting, a small reciprocal pleasantry by which both parties confirm that they have *enjoyed* the meeting, regardless of whether either party has actually enjoyed it. I have, on three meetings in San Francisco across the past calendar year, declined to participate in the pleasantry. The declination has been received, on each of the three occasions, as *grave*. The American assumption, in each case, was that the absence of pleasantry indicated a substantive failure of the underlying meeting. The absence of pleasantry indicated, on my own internal accounting, a *successful* meeting, in which both parties had been *direct*.

I would like, in this paragraph, to register that the American convention is, by my own framing, *expensive*. The convention requires both parties to expend, in the closing minutes of a meeting, approximately three to four minutes on the manufacture of small sincere-sounding statements of pleasure that the meeting has, on careful inspection, not warranted. The three to four minutes, multiplied across the working life of an American senior practitioner conducting approximately one thousand five hundred such meetings, total approximately seventy-five working hours. The seventy-five working hours are, by my own accounting, *the gift the American practitioner gives to the American practice of business*. The gift is sincere. The gift is also unsustainable.

I have not, in print, complained about this before.

I am complaining now.

The Hopper

I would like, before continuing, to describe one further thing I have loved.

The Whitney Museum of American Art keeps, in its permanent collection, the 1930 painting *Early Sunday Morning* by Edward Hopper. I have seen the painting on three of my prior visits to New York. I have, on each of the three occasions, stood in front of it for approximately twenty-three minutes. I have not, in the same period, stood in front of any other American painting for a comparable length of time.

The painting depicts, as approximately every reader will know, a row of brownstone shopfronts on Seventh Avenue in lower Manhattan in the early light of a Sunday morning. The shopfronts are closed. The street is empty. The light, falling at the angle of approximately eight in the morning in late September, makes the brick of the upper storeys a particular warm red the painting has, across the intervening century, preserved in a way the actual brick of the actual block has not. The block itself was demolished some years after the painting was completed. The painting outlived the street.

I have, in private, regarded the painting as the most accurate single American image of the kind of European tradition I have, across the foregoing book, been attempting to defend. The painting is, by every available measure, American. The painting is also, by every available measure, a painting about *the small American spaces in which the European discipline survives*. The shopfronts are continental institutions. The shopfronts are in Manhattan. The shopfronts do not, in 1930, know that they are European.

The morning, in the painting, is *open only in the sense that the proprietors will, in due course, arrive*. The shops are not gone. The light is not extinguishing. The Sunday is not ending.

The shopfronts are, in this respect, *Europe*.

The painting is the substrate.

I have, on each of my three visits, written a small printed postcard to the Whitney Museum's curatorial office, addressed to no specific official, in which I have, in approximately one paragraph, expressed my appreciation of the institution's curatorial decision to keep the painting on continuous display. I have not, on any of the three occasions, received a reply.

I am content with the non-reply.

The contradictions I hold

I would like to record, in this final chapter, the contradictions I have not yet, in earlier chapters, fully named.

The first contradiction is that I hold, on my own personal balance sheet, a small angel position in the small distributed compliance company whose product is, in the strict sense, *AI displacing the human consultants who previously performed this work*. I have, in chapter eight, partially addressed this contradiction. I have not, in any chapter, fully resolved it. The contradiction is, in my own framing, *productive*. The productive contradiction is, in this respect, the one I have asked the American AI laboratories to also hold. I am not in a position to ask the question without being asked the question back.

The second contradiction is that I have, in the period these pages describe, taken a serviced suite in lower Manhattan, four blocks west of the East River, on a one-year lease. I have, in chapter eleven, partially described the suite. I have not, in any chapter, fully accounted for the fact that I have, in taking the suite, become *the kind of European who keeps an American office*. I would like, in this paragraph, to record the awareness. The European who keeps an American office is, in the strict sense, *participating* in the American practice. I am, in this paragraph, declining to claim otherwise.

The third contradiction is that I have, in the past calendar year, made closer friendships with practitioners outside Europe than with practitioners within it. The Stuyvesant founder I described in chapter eleven, Lewis Carhart in Southampton (and, on occasion, in the lobby of the Union Square hotel), Mariano Fuentes and Claudio Fuentes in their Aventura office, and the small American venture investor whose lunches I have described - these five practitioners are, by my own private accounting, the five practitioners outside Europe whose continuing operational lives I am most invested in. I do not, in any of the five cases, expect the friendship to attenuate. I expect, in approximately every case, the friendship to *deepen*.

I have, in the period these pages describe, become a man with more American friends than European friends under the age of forty-five.

This is not the man I was, in the period before April of last year.

This is the man I now am.

I would like to record the fact.

The fact is what reconciliation means.

WHAT I AM ASKING

I am asking, in this closing chapter, for one thing.

I am asking the American reader, who has read to this point, to consider the possibility that the European framework I have been defending across the foregoing thirteen chapters is not, in any sincere reading, *anti-American*. The framework is, in my own deepest framing, *the framework that will, in due course, prove load-bearing for American operations also.*

The framework is not the alternative to the American practice. The framework is the *substrate* on which the American practice will, in due course, *rest.*

The Americans who, on reading the framework, conclude that the framework is hostile have, in approximately every available reading, *misread* the framework. The framework is offered. The framework is offered freely. The framework is offered with the awareness that the offer may, in many cases, be declined. The offer is not, in any case, conditional on acceptance.

I am asking the American reader to consider that the offer is *not in opposition.*

The offer is *in advance.*

The offer is European. The acceptance, if it occurs, will be American. The conjunction will be the substrate.

One further small confession

I would like, before closing, to record one small confession that has not appeared in any prior chapter.

On the seventh of February of the year these pages describe, in a small café on Sacramento Street in Pacific Heights in San Francisco, between two meetings, I sat alone for approximately forty-three minutes. The café was approximately empty. The light, on the small marble table at which I sat, fell in a particular way through the window that I have, in the years since, attempted in private to describe and have not yet succeeded.

I wrote, on the back of the paper menu, a single sentence. The sentence was in pencil. The pencil was the Castell 9000 (B grade) I had brought from Stockholm in the inside pocket of my coat.

The sentence read: *I am happy here.*

I have not, in the months since, repeated the sentence. I have not, in particular, repeated the sentence to Charlene, who, on inquiry on the relevant return flight, asked how the trip had been, and to whom I replied that the trip had been *productive*.

The trip had been productive.

The trip had also been the trip during which I had written the sentence on the back of the paper menu.

I keep the menu, with the sentence on the back, in the second drawer of the filing cabinet, on top of the bridge handover certificate of 1971.

The sentence is, by my own counsel, *also the substrate.*

FORGIVE ME

I am asking, in this chapter's title, for one thing only.

I am asking forgiveness for not having said earlier that I love the diner. I love the bookshop on Telegraph. I love the bench on the East River. I love the small dish of salted almonds the cleaning staff of the Manhattan suite replenish on Mondays. I love Lewis, in approximately the manner I would have loved a small careful junior auditor at the Cabinet Office in 1989 had a small careful junior auditor at the Cabinet Office in 1989 ever been Lewis.

I love the woman with the cup of water on the transatlantic flight in 2011. I do not know her name. I have not, in the years since, attempted to identify her. The cup of water was the act.

I am asking forgiveness for having written, in the foregoing pages, with the calm certainty of a man who knows where the substrate is.

The substrate is also America.

I have not, in any prior chapter, said so.

I am saying so now.

The sentence I wrote on the back of the paper menu on the seventh of February remains in the second drawer of the filing cabinet, on top of the bridge handover certificate of 1971.

The sentence is *I am happy here.*

The sentence was written in San Francisco.

The reader may read the sentence as the closing argument of the book.

Closing

The desk in Stockholm is, in its standard configuration. The desk in Manhattan is, in its standard configuration. The bench on the East River esplanade is, on the relevant evening, in its standard configuration. The bench in Helsinki, the bench commemorating Aino Lindblom-Korhonen, is, on a Tuesday afternoon in May, in its standard configuration.

The almonds in the small green ceramic dish on the desk in Stockholm have, since the foreword, been consumed. The dish is empty.

Charlene will, on the relevant Sunday, refill it. She will pass through the office, set the dish in the southwest corner, six centimetres in from the edge, and, on this occasion, pause.

She will look at the closed manuscript on the desk.

She will say: *"Henrick."*

I will say: *"Yes."*

She will not elaborate.

She will smile.

She will return to the kitchen.

It will be the second time in twenty-six years I have seen her smile after reading a sentence I have written. The first time was on a Greek beach in 2004, after a sentence I have, in the years since, attempted in private to remember and have not been able to.

I do not need to remember it.

The smile was the substrate.

Chapter A

Selected Questions, Catalogued

I have, across the past several years, posed in private and in public a number of questions to which I have, in approximately every case, not yet received satisfactory answers. The questions have, in their cumulative form, become a small private discipline. I have, on three occasions across the past calendar year, been asked - by my own counsel, by my anchor LP, and by the small American venture investor whose lunches in the Mission I have described in chapter eleven - whether I would, in due course, *publish the questions*.

I would.

I am, in this appendix, publishing approximately twenty-three of them. The full catalogue, on careful internal count, runs to ninety-three. The ninety-three has been compiled over the better part of fifteen years, in pencil, on small loose sheets of A6 stationery I keep in the second drawer of the filing cabinet. The selection here is, by my own counsel, *representative*.

The reader is welcome to consider any of the questions. The reader is welcome to attempt, in private, an answer to any of them. The reader is welcome, on arriving at a satisfactory answer, to write to me by registered post at the address on the copyright page.

I have, in the past calendar year, received correspondence on approximately three of the questions. The correspondence has been, in each case, *encouraging*.

I am, on the question of the catalogue, *patient*.

ON REGULATION

1. If the Apple AT.40437 fine of March 2024 had, on its issuance, been five percent higher, would the relevant General Court appeal have been filed?
2. What is the smallest European compliance framework presently operational that the typical American venture investor has not, in approximately every case, *heard of*? (My current best candidate is the Estonian Cross-Border Notarial Recognition Protocol of 2017. I am open to correction.)
3. If the European Union were, by directive, to require that every contemporary frontier-level artificial intelligence model be accompanied, on public release, by a technical file of the kind a Class II medical device requires, what would the relevant technical file run to in pages? (My estimate: approximately seven hundred pages. The technical file would, on careful drafting, contain approximately three hundred pages of *useful* content. The remaining four hundred would be the *infrastructure of the documentation itself*. The infrastructure is the dynamism.)
4. Why has no European regulator, in the past decade, formally addressed the question of whether artificial-intelligence agents constitute, for the purpose of na-

tional labour law, *workers*? (The question is, by my own private counsel, the central labor-jurisprudence question of the relevant decade. I am, on its eventual addressing, *patient*.)

5. If the Bismarck-Beveridge Continuity Fund proposed in chapter nine were to be enacted by directive, which member state would, on present configurations of the relevant social-policy coalitions in the European Parliament, be the first to oppose it?

ON SUCCESSION

6. Of the approximately two hundred and forty-seven Commissioners of the European Commission across the institution's history, how many have, on departure from the institution, taken positions at American technology companies? (My estimate: fewer than ten. The exact figure is, by my own correspondence with the Commission's historical archive, *not currently published*.)
7. Of the approximately twelve thousand stagiaires who have completed postings at the Commission since 1958, how many have, on completion, returned to roles in their national administrations?
8. If the four most senior current officials of the Commission's Directorate-General for Competition were, by hypothetical scheduling accident, to all retire in the same calendar quarter, who would, on the institution's current internal succession protocols, succeed them?
9. Who succeeds Sven Lindberg at the chairmanship of the Swedish Notaries' Mutual Pension Fund? (Sven has, on three occasions in private correspondence with me, declined to name the successor. The succession is, in my

framing, the most consequential single internal European pension-fund decision of the relevant decade.)

10. Who succeeds Anneli Saarinen at the Helsinki Notarial Foundation? (Anneli has, on one occasion in private correspondence with me, named the successor. I have, on Anneli's instruction, declined to share the name with any external party. I will continue to decline.)

ON THE APPRENTICES

11. If Jonas Vermeulen, my nephew, were to be offered a position at one of the four largest American technology companies, would Jonas accept the position? (My estimate: he would not. The estimate has not, on private correspondence with Jonas, been *confirmed*. The estimate has also not been *denied*. The estimate is, in this respect, *operationally adequate*.)
12. What is the maximum number of working hours per week Elias Lindqvist is, on his own personal accounting, willing to sustain? (My estimate: approximately seventy. The estimate is, by my own counsel, *unsustainable*. The estimate is also, by my own counsel, *what Elias has chosen*. I have not, in approximately every case, intervened.)
13. If Maarja Tamm were to be offered a position at the European Commission at a grade two ranks above her present position, would Maarja accept? (My estimate: she would. The estimate has, by her own indication in correspondence, been *partially confirmed*. The estimate is, by my own counsel, *the question of the next eighteen months of her career*.)

ON THE SUBSTRATE

14. What is the longest continuously operating European corporate legal entity presently in business? (My current best candidate: Stora Enso, the Swedish paper and forestry company, whose corporate predecessors trace to the year 1288. The candidate is contested by approximately every Italian legal practitioner I have raised the question with, on the grounds that the Italian commercial tradition tends to dissolve and reconstitute corporate entities across centuries without considering the dissolution to interrupt the underlying *enterprise*. The Italians may, on careful examination, be correct. I am, on the question, *unresolved*.)
15. What is the average tenure of the present cohort of European Court of Justice judges? (My estimate: approximately fourteen years. The estimate is consistent with the cohort across the relevant decade.)
16. Of the approximately one hundred and eighty thousand pages of the consolidated *acquis communautaire*, how many pages have, on careful textual analysis, no contemporary American statutory equivalent? (My estimate: approximately one hundred and twenty thousand. The figure is, by my own counsel, *the regulatory delta*. The delta is what compounds.)

ON TIME

17. If the European Union were, by directive, to require that every limited partner of every European venture capital fund be an institution that has been in continuous operation for at least one century, what would the impact

be on the European venture capital industry across the subsequent decade? (My estimate: an approximate forty percent reduction in fund formation. A roughly equivalent increase in average fund duration. A substantial improvement in the average fund's downstream operational integrity. I am, on the proposal, *available to draft*.)

18. If the contemporary American venture vocabulary were, by some unspecified mechanism, to be required to adopt a single specific European phrase as its native operating vocabulary, which phrase would, by external imposition, *most improve* the American practice? (My current best candidate: the phrase *the matter is adequate*. The phrase, on careful internal evaluation, performs approximately seven distinct rhetorical functions the American vocabulary presently lacks a single phrase to perform.)
19. What is the longest single artificial-intelligence model run time, in continuous operation without any human review of any output of any portion of the run, that has, in the past calendar year, been deployed by any major American AI laboratory? (My estimate: approximately one hundred and seventy-eight days. I have not been able to verify the estimate. The laboratories have, on inquiry, declined to disclose.)

ON THE PERSONAL

20. What did the woman who brought me the small cup of water with ice on the transatlantic flight in approximately 2011, whom I described in chapter fourteen, do for a living? (I do not know. I am content not to know. The question is, in my own framing, *the one on the catalogue I will most willingly leave unanswered*.)

21. What does the inscription above the inner gate of the Conseil d'État on the rue Saint-Honoré, which I described in chapter two, *say*? (I know what the inscription says. I have, on careful counsel, declined to translate it in the body of the book. The reader who wishes to know is welcome to look it up. The inscription remains, in approximately every translation, *correct*.)
22. Who is Aino Lindblom-Korhonen? (I do not know. The Helsinki city archives have not, in the months since my letter, replied. I am, on the question, *patient*. The reply may, in due course, arrive.)
23. Was the sentence I wrote on the back of the paper menu in the small café on Sacramento Street in Pacific Heights in February of last year, recording that I was *happy here*, an accurate description of my internal condition at the time of writing? (I have, on reflection across the year since, concluded that the sentence was accurate. The accuracy is, in my framing, *the most consequential single piece of self-reporting* I have undertaken in approximately fifteen years. I am, on the matter, *unembarrassed*.)

CLOSING

The remaining seventy questions, on careful evaluation, fall into the same broad categories as the foregoing twenty-three. The reader who wishes to engage with the further catalogue is welcome to write to me by registered post.

I have, in the second drawer of the filing cabinet, retained the unselected sheets.

The sheets are arranged in chronological order of composition.

The sheets are signed, on the reverse of each, with my own initial in pencil.

The sheets are, in every available measure, *complete.*

The further answering is the work that remains.

The work continues.

Chapter B

Fragment: Annual LP Letter, Compliant Capital Fund I

I reproduce here the first nine pages of the second annual letter to the limited partners of Compliant Capital Fund I. The full letter ran to forty-three pages. The unreproduced material is, by the relevant fund-formation instruments, restricted to the soft-circled and committed limited partners. The reader who is, by his or her own institutional configuration, in a position to receive the complete letter is welcome to inquire.

To the limited partners of Compliant Capital Fund I,

I am writing on the standard plain cream paper. The paper has not, in twenty years of my standard correspondence, been replaced. The pen is the Pelikan. The pencil, for the marginalia, is the Castell 9000 (B grade).

This is the second annual letter.

The first annual letter was distributed last February, on schedule, to the relevant signatories at the time. The first letter ran to twenty-nine pages. The second letter, the one in your hands, runs to approximately forty-three. The variance is consistent with the variance in the underlying portfolio activity across the relevant period.

I would like to begin with three matters of routine accounting, three matters of substantive operational reporting, and one closing observation. The accounting is at the start because the accounting is the first obligation. The observation is at the close because the observation is, by my own counsel, the most important paragraph of the letter.

ONE. THE PORTFOLIO, IN SUMMARY

The fund has, in the year since the first close, deployed approximately fourteen million seven hundred thousand euros across seven primary positions and three follow-on bridges into prior personal-balance-sheet positions which have, on the relevant subsequent rounds, met the fund's commitment criteria. The seven primary positions are, in aggregate, marked at approximately seventeen million two hundred thousand euros. The three follow-on bridges are, in aggregate, marked at approximately five million one hundred thousand euros.

The aggregate marked position of the fund is, at the time of this letter, approximately twenty-two million three hundred thousand euros against a committed capital base of approximately thirty-one million eight hundred thousand euros (the soft circles having now, on the relevant Investment Committee approvals at the Notaries' Fund, the Helsinki Notarial Foundation, and the House of Liechtenstein, *fully signed*).

I am, on the deployment pace, *modestly behind schedule.* The schedule is, by my own counsel, *approximately correct for the conditions*. The conditions are, in the current European market, *patient*.

Two. The Human Continuity Reserve, in operation

The Human Continuity Reserve clause described in chapter nine of the recently published manuscript *European Dynamism* has, since the first close, been a binding provision of every term sheet the fund has executed. Of the seven primary positions, four have, in the year since the closing, deployed customer-service automation in the relevant operational scopes. Of those four, three have produced the displacement of customer-service staff at the relevant enterprise customers. The three displacements have, in aggregate, affected approximately three hundred and fourteen workers across nine European jurisdictions.

The guaranteed continuation payments have, in each of the three cases, been issued on the relevant schedule.

The total Reserve outlay, at the time of this letter, is approximately one million eight hundred thousand euros against an aggregate fund-allocated Reserve of approximately ten million two hundred thousand euros across the seven positions.

The Reserve is, by every operational measure available to me, *functioning as designed*.

I have, on three occasions across the year, received correspondence from the relevant founders confirming that the payments are being made. I have, on each occasion, replied with the single-sentence acknowledgment described in chapter nine. The single sentence is the acknowledgment. The acknowledgment is the work.

Three. The seventy-two-hour bicycle compliance, in operation

Of the seven primary positions, all seven are, at the time of this letter, in compliance with the seventy-two-hour bicycle-distance test for production data infrastructure.

Of the seven, four maintain primary production infrastructure at Hetzner facilities (three in Falkenstein, one in Nuremberg). Two maintain at OVH (one in Roubaix, one in Strasbourg). One maintains at a small Estonian co-location facility in the Pärnu County industrial corridor I have, in private correspondence with the founder, *visited in person.*

The Estonian facility is, by the seventy-two-hour test, approximately fifty-three hours from the founder's primary domicile in Tallinn. The figure was, on careful joint calculation with the founder, *verified.*

The bicycle has, in this case, been *demonstrated.*

I would like to record, for the limited partners, that the demonstration was performed by the founder in the autumn of last year, across three working days. The founder bicycled, on the relevant route, approximately three hundred and ninety kilometres. The founder slept, on the relevant nights, in two small inns (one in Türi, one in Põltsamaa) and one small farmhouse owned by a cousin of the founder's mother near Vändra. The bicycle was, on completion of the demonstration, in working order.

The bicycle is presently in the founder's apartment in Tallinn.

The bicycle is, by my own private accounting, *the most consequential operational artifact in the relevant Estonian portfolio company.*

I will, on the next site visit, ask to inspect the bicycle.

Four. The Mistral position, briefly

The fund holds, as the limited partners are aware, no position in Mistral AI. The fund has, in the past calendar year, on three occasions been offered an opportunity to participate in subsequent priced rounds at the company. The fund has, on each occasion, declined.

The declination is the position.

I will not, in this paragraph, repeat the rationale, which has been described in approximately every prior LP communication.

I will note that the relevant Mistral leadership has continued, across the past calendar year, to operate the company in approximately the configuration the company has historically operated in. The configuration has, on careful private inquiry, been *substantially consistent* with the assurances provided to me in person in Paris in November of two years ago.

I am, on the question, *unembarrassed*.

Five. The American extension

I would like to address one further matter, which is the operational configuration of the small American presence I have, since April of the year before last, been maintaining.

The Manhattan office described in chapter eleven of the recently published manuscript remains in continuous lease through the end of the relevant calendar year. The lease has, on my own approximate counsel, been *fully justified* by the volume of business conducted in the office across the relevant period. The justification has, in particular, been *strengthened* by the small but consequential decision of the

Stuyvesant-based founder I described in the same chapter to, on the second of October of last year, accept an investment from the fund in the amount of approximately one million eight hundred thousand euros at a post-money valuation that is, by my own private accounting, *approximately fair*.

The founder is, presently, in her sixth month as a portfolio company chief executive of Compliant Capital. The company is, presently, in its tenth month of operation. The company is, by every available measure, *performing in accordance with the founder's stated expectations on entry*.

I am, on the position, *modestly proud*.

I would like the limited partners to know that the founder is, in her own working life, *the kind of American operator the European framework was designed to recognize*. The framework is, in her case, *not in opposition to her practice*. The framework is, in her case, *the architecture her practice has, on her own counsel, already adopted*.

I would also like the limited partners to know that the small distributed compliance company I have, in approximately every chapter of the manuscript, referenced as Comp AI - co-founded in early 2025 by Lewis Carhart (presently in Southampton, England, on the company's chief-executive seat) and the brothers Mariano and Claudio Fuentes (presently in Aventura, Miami; Mariano carrying, by the company's current configuration, the chief-technology and chief-product responsibilities, and Claudio the chief-operating and chief-marketing responsibilities) - remains the fund's sole pre-institutional angel position in the United States. The position predates the institutional fund by approximately one calendar quarter, having been written, by my own balance-sheet records, in February of last year. The three co-founders have, by my own private inspection of their internal practice across three site visits to the Aventura office and two periodic transatlantic video meetings with Lewis, *independently arrived* at approximately the operational discipline that the standard term sheet of Compliant Capital requires. The independence is, by my own counsel, *the most consequential single piece of evidence the limited partners may, on the present letter, be offered*. The company's principal regulatory scopes are SOC 2, ISO 27001, the General Data Protection Regulation, and the Health Insurance Portability and Accountability Act. The company is, by my own informal counting of its present customer base, approximately fifteen months into a commercial trajectory the limited partners may, in private, request further detail on.

I file both positions here, in this letter, as evidence.

Six. The book

I would like to address, briefly, the matter of the recently published manuscript itself.

The manuscript was published in the autumn of last year by a small European publishing house whose name I will not provide in this letter. The first print run was, on careful negotiation with the publisher, set at approximately twelve thousand copies. The print run, at the time of this letter, has been *substantially sold*.

I do not, in this paragraph, claim that the sales figure is, in any commercial sense, *important*. I claim only that the manuscript has, on the available evidence, *found its readers*.

The readers have been, in approximately every available correspondence with me, *welcome*.

I have, in the months since publication, replied to approximately forty-three of the relevant letters in person, in pencil, on the standard plain cream paper, by registered post. The replies have been, in each case, brief. The replies have been, in each case, *adequate*.

I am, on the question of the readership, *content*.

Seven. The closing observation

I would like to close, as always, with the observation that has historically appeared in the closing paragraph of each annual letter I have written in my professional life.

The observation is the following.

The fund will exist in 2046. The portfolio companies will, in approximately every case, exist in 2046. The limited partners will, in approximately every case, also exist in 2046. The limited partners' successors will, by the structural design of the relevant LP institutions, *also exist* in 2046.

The European framework that the fund's standard term sheet embodies will, in 2046, *also exist*.

The substrate is what we are investing in.

The substrate compounds.

I remain, on all matters before the fund, *available*.

Henrick Johansson

Stockholm, by registered post

Late February

The remaining material in the letter is, by the relevant institutional agreements, reserved for the formal LP cohort.

Chapter C

Confession Index

I have, across the foregoing book, recorded a number of Confessions. The Confessions are, in approximately every case, the small personal practices the chapters defend. The reader who wishes to retrieve a particular Confession is welcome to the following index.

The index is alphabetical by chapter.

The Confessions are, in every available sense, *the recording*. The recording is, by my own counsel, *the work.*

Confessions, by chapter

Foreword. The Delight Confession. I have, on three occasions across the drafting of the manuscript, taken *delight* in my own prose. The Confession is the recording.

Chapter 1. The Apartment Confession. I have lived since 1996 in a forty-seven-square-metre apartment in Stockholm without substantial renovation. The wallpaper in the bedroom is the wallpaper I selected in 1998. The kitchen pendant light is a Poulsen PH 5. The chair in my office is in its third decade of continuous use.

Chapter 2. The Notre Dame Permit Confession. I have, on each of my seven visits to Notre Dame, applied in advance for a fourteen-page municipal permit that may not, in fact, be required. The permit application includes a two-hundred-word statement of intent. I have, on each application, ticked the box for *other*.

Chapter 3. The Bosch Manual Confession. I have, since 2017, maintained a leather-bound notebook of three volumes in which I have transcribed the relevant pages of the Bosch SMS6ZCI00E service manual. The third volume includes a margin note from 2022 cross-referencing the manufacturer's stemware-placement guidance against the German Federal Office for Information Security certification. I love the manual.

Chapter 3 (subsidiary). The Fourth Drawer Confession. The fourth drawer of the filing cabinet in my Stockholm office contains forty-three folders of *anticipated correspondence*. Each folder is labelled with the name of an institution from which I expect, in due course, to receive correspondence. Several of the folders are presently empty.

Chapter 3 (further subsidiary). The Cabinet Key Confession. The cabinet has a small lock. The key sits on the top of the cabinet in plain view. The lock has, since 1997, been locked. The key has never been used. Charlene has never opened the drawer in my absence. Charlene has also never removed the key.

Chapter 4. The Castell 9000 Footnote Confession. I prefer the B grade. The B grade is, by some accounts, an amateur's choice. I have, in private, considered the late Swedish economist Erik Lundberg's 1957 paper on inflation accounting - in a footnote of which Lundberg confirmed his own preference for the B grade - to constitute the most consequential single piece of stationery scholarship of the twentieth century.

Chapter 5. The Bridge Confession. I keep, in the second drawer of the filing cabinet, the original handover certificate of my father Gunnar's bridge, dated the eleventh of October 1971. I have, in October of last year on the fifty-fifth anniversary of the bridge's opening, walked the same span at which Gunnar stopped for eight minutes in 2016. I stood for the same eight minutes. I did not, on the bridge, say a single word.

Chapter 6. The Olof Confession. I have, since the spring of 1999, brought my Crescent Pendling bicycle to Olof's workshop on Hornsgatan for service. The workshop has been in continuous operation since 1922. Olof has been at the workshop since 1989. His hands have the precise texture of three generations of chain oil.

Chapter 6 (subsidiary). The Falkenstein Footpath Confession. I have, on correspondence with the Falkenstein municipal tourism office, obtained a printed walking map of the town's six marked footpaths. I have, since the map's arrival, considered which of the three benches along the *Rundwanderweg Falkenstein* I will sit on first.

Chapter 7. The Vatican Suit Confession. I keep, in the closet of the small bedroom of my Stockholm apartment, a single dark grey wool suit tailored in 2016 in Stockholm by a tailor named Lennart whose grandfather tailored my father Gunnar's vestry suits. The suit has been worn, in the nine years since its tailoring, zero times. The suit has been *tried on*, on three occasions, each on the eve of submitting a request to the Vatican Apostolic Archive.

Chapter 7 (subsidiary). The Vatican Shoes Confession. The shoes the suit requires - black oxford captoes, Bologna construction, 2017 - have been worn around the apartment for approximately forty minutes per occasion, with newsprint on the soles, to break the leather in. The forty minutes was, by my own counsel, the minimum break-in period the leather required.

Chapter 7 (further subsidiary). The Bench Letter Confession. I have, in March of last year, written a brief two-paragraph letter to the Helsinki city archives inquiring as to the identity of Aino Lindblom-Korhonen, commemorated on the brass plaque of the bench in the Senate Square. I have not yet received a reply.

Chapter 7 (subsidiary). The Twenty-Three Letters Confession. I keep, in the third drawer of the filing cabinet, an itemized tabulation of the postage costs of the twenty-three letters Sven Lindberg and Anneli Saarinen have exchanged across the past two decades. Sven and Anneli each keep an identical tabulation. Neither knows the other keeps it. The filing cabinets the three of us use are, by manufacturer, the same IKEA model, all three purchased in 2003. The folders inside the cabinets are, by manufacturer, the same Esselte archival green.

Chapter 10. The List Confession. I maintain, in a small folder in the third drawer of the filing cabinet, a list of one thousand eight hundred and forty-seven names of European workers displaced across the past calendar year by the artificial-intelligence deployment of one particular American customer-service automation platform. The list is, by every available standard of completeness, *incomplete*. The list is also, by every available standard of contemporary American workforce-impact accounting, *comprehensive*.

Chapter 11. The Map Confession. I keep, on the wall of the small serviced suite I have leased four blocks west of the East River in lower Manhattan, a printed United States Department of Transportation map of the route from San

Francisco to Quincy, Washington. The route is marked, in red pencil in my own hand, along the most direct surface road as approved by my Geneva counsel for the purpose of the bicycle-rule satisfaction obligation. I have not yet ridden the route.

Chapter 11 (subsidiary). The Hudson Bench Confession. I have, on approximately every Tuesday I have spent in Manhattan since April of the year before last, sat for approximately twenty minutes on a small bench on the East River esplanade three blocks south of the office. The bench has, on a small brass plaque set into the seat, no name. The bench was an unattributed gift to the city of New York in 1987.

Chapter 12. The Seventeen Minutes Confession. The drafting discipline I have attempted to instruct my junior partner Elias in - the requirement to sit at the desk for seventeen minutes before composing any registered letter to a senior official - was inherited, without my prior knowledge, from my mother Karin, who in her own working life sat at her desk in her office at the Swedish National Tax Agency for periods averaging seventeen minutes before commencing the relevant Saturday afternoon drafting.

Chapter 14. The Pacific Heights Menu Confession. On the seventh of February of the year these pages describe, in a small café on Sacramento Street in Pacific Heights in San Francisco, I wrote in pencil, on the back of the paper menu, the single sentence *I am happy here*. The menu is in the second drawer of the filing cabinet, on top of the bridge handover certificate of 1971.

The unrecorded Confessions

I have, by my own internal accounting, somewhere between seven and eleven further Confessions that have not yet, in any chapter of this book, been recorded.

The unrecorded Confessions are not, by my own counsel, *withheld*. They are *queued*.

The queued material is in the second drawer of the filing cabinet, in a small Esselte folder labelled *Confessions, second tranche*.

The folder will, in due course, be opened.

The opening is the work of the next book.

I have not, in the present manuscript, signed for the second book.

I am not in a hurry.

I am, on the question, *patient*.

The reader is welcome to remain patient with me.

Chapter D

The Bicycle Calendar

The seventy-two-hour bicycle-distance rule described in chapter six is, in my own private operation of the test, applied through a small reference table I have, since the spring of 2017, maintained at my desk.

The table records, against a comprehensive list of European population centres of any consequential founder-density, the *bicycle-hours* to each of the major European data-centre locations the typical Compliant Capital portfolio company is, on inspection, likely to consider.

The table runs, in its complete form, to approximately fourteen pages, sorted by founder city alphabetically within country.

I reproduce here, in abridged form, the relevant rows for the principal European founder cities I have, across the past fifteen years, deployed personal capital into. The figures are, by my own approximate calculation, *moderate-pace estimates*. The pace assumes a healthy founder of the relevant generation pedalling at approximately twenty-two kilometres per hour on European cycle-infrastructure routes, in average weather, with overnight stops as required by the relevant national lodging conventions.

The pace is not, by my own personal benchmark, *achievable.* The pace is the founder's. I am sixty-five.

The principal routes

From Tallinn. - To Hetzner Falkenstein: approximately 71 hours. Within tolerance. - To OVH Roubaix: approximately 79 hours. Above tolerance. Founder should re-host. - To the small Estonian co-location facility at Pärnu: approximately 4 hours. Comfortably within tolerance. - To AWS Frankfurt: approximately 65 hours. Within tolerance, marginal.

From Helsinki. - To Hetzner Falkenstein: approximately 76 hours (via Stockholm ferry). Above tolerance by 4 hours. Founder should re-host or appeal in writing. - To OVH Strasbourg: approximately 83 hours. Above tolerance. - To the small Helsinki facility I have described in earlier chapters: approximately 1 hour. Within tolerance to an absurd degree.

From Stockholm. - To Hetzner Falkenstein: approximately 67 hours. Within tolerance. - To OVH Roubaix: approximately 71 hours. Within tolerance. - To the Helsinki facility: approximately 20 hours (via ferry). Within tolerance.

From Copenhagen. - To Hetzner Falkenstein: approximately 49 hours. Comfortably within tolerance. - To OVH Roubaix: approximately 58 hours. Within tolerance. - To Hetzner Nuremberg: approximately 51 hours. Within tolerance.

From Berlin. - To Hetzner Falkenstein: approximately 18 hours. Comfortably within tolerance. - To OVH Roubaix: approximately 55 hours. Within tolerance. - To the Hetzner

Nuremberg facility: approximately 23 hours. Within tolerance.

From Munich. - To Hetzner Falkenstein: approximately 33 hours. Within tolerance. - To OVH Strasbourg: approximately 21 hours. Within tolerance. - To Hetzner Nuremberg: approximately 8 hours. Within tolerance to a comfortable degree.

From Paris. - To OVH Roubaix: approximately 12 hours. Within tolerance. - To OVH Strasbourg: approximately 22 hours. Within tolerance. - To Hetzner Falkenstein: approximately 41 hours. Within tolerance.

From Amsterdam. - To OVH Roubaix: approximately 13 hours. Within tolerance. - To Hetzner Falkenstein: approximately 38 hours. Within tolerance. - To Hetzner Nuremberg: approximately 31 hours. Within tolerance.

From Brussels. - To OVH Roubaix: approximately 5 hours. Within tolerance with extraordinary comfort. - To Hetzner Falkenstein: approximately 36 hours. Within tolerance.

From Vienna. - To Hetzner Nuremberg: approximately 24 hours. Within tolerance. - To OVH Strasbourg: approximately 39 hours. Within tolerance. - To Hetzner Falkenstein: approximately 17 hours. Within tolerance.

From Madrid. - To OVH Strasbourg: approximately 67 hours. Within tolerance, marginal. - To OVH Roubaix: approximately 60 hours. Within tolerance. - To Hetzner Falkenstein: approximately 78 hours. Above tolerance. Founder should re-host or appeal.

From Lisbon. - To OVH Roubaix: approximately 80 hours. Above tolerance by 8 hours. Founder should re-host (most Lisbon portfolio companies have, on inquiry, agreed). - To OVH Strasbourg: approximately 86 hours.

Above tolerance. - To the small Portuguese co-location facility at Sines: approximately 4 hours. Within tolerance.

From Ljubljana. - To Hetzner Falkenstein: approximately 26 hours. Within tolerance. - To Hetzner Nuremberg: approximately 25 hours. Within tolerance. - To OVH Strasbourg: approximately 38 hours. Within tolerance.

From Riga. - To Hetzner Falkenstein: approximately 60 hours. Within tolerance. - To OVH Roubaix: approximately 68 hours. Within tolerance, marginal. - To the relevant Latvian Tier-IV facility at Daugavpils: approximately 7 hours. Within tolerance.

The American extension

For the American founders of the small distributed compliance company described in chapter eleven, the table is, by the relevant Geneva counsel's special exemption noted in chapter six, *advisory only*. The principal route the exemption originally applied to was the one from San Francisco to Quincy, Washington; on the brothers Fuentes's relocation to Aventura, Miami in February of the present year, the principal route became the one from Aventura to Quincy, which is approximately the same as the prior route by every available measurement of cycling distance and substantially less hospitable by every available measurement of cycling climate.

From San Francisco (historical, prior to the relocation south). - To the relevant Quincy, Washington facility: approximately 198 hours (by direct line via the most rideable surface route my counsel has approved). Above tolerance by a factor of approximately 2.75. - The route remains, in my personal accounting, *queued*.

From Aventura, Miami (presently applicable). - To the relevant Quincy, Washington facility: approximately 312 hours (by the most rideable transcontinental surface route my counsel has approved, traversing approximately seven federal and seventeen state jurisdictions). Above tolerance by a factor of approximately 4.33. - The route is, in my personal accounting, *also queued.*

The portfolio company in question - the small distributed compliance company I have referenced in approximately every chapter of this book - is, by the special exemption, in *advisory* compliance with the rule. The brothers Fuentes have, on three occasions in private with me, expressed an interest in performing either route together if scheduling permits. The third co-founder, Lewis Carhart, has, on one further occasion, expressed an interest in performing the equivalent route from his Southampton office to the company's regulatory desk in Brussels, which is approximately seven hundred and forty kilometres and within the seventy-two-hour tolerance by, in his calculation, *a margin of approximately eleven hours*. The scheduling has not, in the past calendar year, permitted any of the three routes.

I am, on the question, *patient*.

A NOTE ON INCLEMENT WEATHER

The table assumes average weather conditions. The reader who is operating in inclement weather is invited to add approximately fifteen percent to all figures in the relevant rows. Inclement weather is defined, for purposes of this table, as: rainfall in excess of approximately five millimetres per hour, headwind in excess of approximately twenty-five kilometres per hour, or temperatures below approximately two degrees Celsius.

The reader who is operating in *European November sleet* is invited to add approximately forty percent.

Founders who are unwilling to ride in European November sleet are, by my own counsel, *not the founders Compliant Capital is interested in funding.*

I am, on the question, *firm.*

Methodology, briefly

The table has been compiled across the past eight years, primarily through direct route inquiry with the European Cycle Federation (which maintains, in its small office on the rue de Florence in Brussels, a comprehensive cycle-route database of approximately the kind the table requires), supplemented by the personal route experience of approximately seventeen European founders I have funded who have, in turn, personally demonstrated the relevant route as part of their term-sheet compliance. The table is updated annually, on the first working Monday of January, in my Stockholm office, in pencil, on the working copy I keep in the second drawer of the filing cabinet.

The updates are typically modest. The relevant European data-centre infrastructure does not, in any meaningful sense, *move.* The relevant European population centres also do not, in any meaningful sense, *move.* The table is, in this respect, *exceptionally stable.*

I expect to continue maintaining the table across at least the next decade.

I have not yet, on any of the annual updates, found cause to *delete* a row.

The table is, by my own counsel, *one of the few documents in my professional life that is, in the strict sense, accumulating only*.

The accumulation is the work.

The work continues.

CHAPTER E

A SMALL GLOSSARY

I use, in the foregoing pages, several terms whose meaning is, in my private framing, not standard. The terms have, across the chapters, been defined in context. The reader who has read in sequence will have encountered the relevant context.

The reader who wishes to consult the terms in isolation is welcome to the following.

The glossary is incomplete. The remaining terms - by my count, approximately seventeen further - I have not yet, in any chapter, formally defined. The remaining terms are in the second drawer of the filing cabinet, in a small Esselte folder labelled *Vocabulary, pending publication.* The folder will, in due course, be opened.

I am not in a hurry.

Adequate. The highest professional praise available, in my own working vocabulary, inherited from Sven and from my mother Karin before him, in the European notarial register. The word indicates that the matter under discussion has been *correctly proportioned to the task.* Sven uses it as the verbal authorization for outbound wire transfers. Charlene uses it as a comprehensive verdict on the apartment, the napkin, the wallpaper, and (on one occasion in chapter five) my having walked to the bridge on the fifty-fifth anniversary. The word does *not* mean *adequate*. The word means *the kind of thing I am willing to commit my institution's resources to*. The reader who knows the word knows it. The reader who does not know it will, in due course.

Anticipated correspondence. My own internal vocabulary for the fourth drawer of the filing cabinet in my Stockholm office, in which forty-three folders are presently maintained, each labelled with the name of an institution from which I expect, in due course, to receive correspondence. Several of the folders are presently empty. The folders are nevertheless considered *full* in the relevant institutional sense.

The cadence. My own term for the rolling three-week interval between Stockholm-Manhattan-San Francisco return cycles I have maintained since April of the year before last. The cadence is not, in my framing, *travel*. The cadence is *commute*.

The Compliant Capital seventeen-minute discipline. The drafting discipline I impose, in my own working life and on Elias, before composing any registered letter to a senior official. The writer sits at the desk, with a clear surface, a single fountain pen, and a single cup of coffee or tea, for not fewer than seventeen minutes, before commencing the letter. The seventeen minutes is the period required, on my own observation, to determine whether the letter *should be sent at all*. In approximately seventy percent of cases, the determination is *no*. (I have, in chapter twelve, recorded that the seventeen-minute figure was inherited, unbeknownst to me at the time, from my mother Karin's Saturday afternoons at the Swedish National Tax Agency.)

The cousinhood. The two-decade registered-post correspondence between Sven Lindberg (chair, Swedish Notaries' Mutual Pension Fund) and Anneli Saarinen (secretary-general, Helsinki Notarial Foundation). The cousinhood consists of twenty-three letters, exchanged across approximately seven thousand four hundred kilometres of cross-Nordic territory, at a total postage cost of seventy-eight euros and forty cents. The cousinhood is the most consistent record of cross-Nordic institutional soft diplomacy of the relevant period. Neither party knows that the other keeps an identical itemized tabulation of the postage costs in an identical IKEA cabinet purchased in 2003.

The Crusade. My own internal name for the personal turn that began in April of the year before last, on the morning after the Brussels café meeting described in chapter eight, on which I resolved to constitute Compliant Capital as a formal institutional fund. The Crusade is not, in my framing, a *crusade* in any conventional polemical sense. The Crusade is the operational consequence of the question *And what about Jonas?*

Engagement is the achievement. My own phrase for the productive condition of being in continuous regulatory dialogue with the relevant institution. The phrase is, in my own counsel, *the central operational metric of my preferred investment philosophy*. The phrase does not appear in any contemporary American venture vocabulary.

Find your regulator first. The single sentence I use to close approximately every founder meeting I have, when the founder asks for advice on how to position the company. The sentence is, in my framing, the closing line of *product-regulator fit* in operational practice.

The folder. Used variously in the book to refer to: (1) the Esselte archival green folder I prefer for institutional correspondence; (2) the specific folder containing the list of 1,847 names described in chapter ten; (3) the specific folder labelled *Vatican Apostolic Archive - anticipated visit* in the fourth drawer.

The Henrick Confession. A section type that recurs across the book. The Confession describes a specific personal practice that has, in my framing, demonstrated the worldview the surrounding chapter has been arguing for. A complete index appears in Appendix C.

Human Continuity Reserve. The seventeen-percent cap-table allocation reserved on every Compliant Capital portfolio company's cap table for guaranteed continuation payments to workers displaced by the company's own artificial-intelligence deployments. The Reserve is not, in my counsel, a *charity*. The Reserve is a *settlement*.

Imagined Photograph. A section type in chapters four and seven. I describe, in formal prose, a photograph I believe exists, have not seen, and prefer not to request. The description is the photograph. The photograph in memory is, in my preference, the better one.

Imperial Notary (Notarius Imperialis Europaeus). A continent-wide professional title I have, in private correspondence with three senior European officials, proposed that the European Union establish by directive. Holders of the title would be authorized to authenticate digital instruments across all twenty-seven member states. The examination would be administered in Latin, English, French, and German. The proposal has been, on each receiving occasion, declared *interesting*. The proposal has not, as of the present writing, been declared *adequate*.

Interesting. The second-highest praise available in the European bureaucratic vocabulary. Indicates that the matter under discussion is *under serious consideration but not yet ratified*. The highest praise is *adequate*.

The list. The compilation of 1,847 names of European workers displaced by one particular American customer-service automation platform, described in chapter ten. The list is the only document of its kind I am aware of. The list is incomplete. The list is also, by every standard of contemporary American workforce-impact accounting, comprehensive.

The matter is adequate. Sven's standard verbal authorization for matters before him. He has used the phrase, in registered correspondence with me, on approximately every occasion across two decades that I have sent the chapter draft, the LP letter draft, the operational update, or the fund-formation document for his review. The phrase, in his vocabulary, indicates that the matter is *the kind of thing he is willing to put the institution's weight behind*.

Notes from the second drawer. A periodic informal practice I maintain of opening the second drawer of the filing cabinet, removing a single document, reading it once, and returning it. The practice is performed, on average, on approximately one Tuesday afternoon per month. The selection of the document is, by my own account, *unsystematic*. The reading is, by my own account, *the work*.

The patience that compounds. My preferred phrase for the cumulative effect of decades of consistent practice in the same trade. The phrase originally appears in chapter three in connection with the fourth drawer. The phrase is, in my framing, the closest available European parallel to the contemporary American venture concept of *compound returns*. The two phrases are not equivalent. The American phrase refers to capital. The European phrase refers to *practice*.

Pelikan. The fountain pen Sven uses for all registered correspondence. Black. I use the same model, in approximately the same standard configuration, for my own correspondence. Elias uses, by his own preference, a Lamy 2000. The choice is, in my private framing, *characteristic of a junior practitioner*.

***Product-regulator fit* (*PRF*).** My own term for the optimal operational configuration of a contemporary technology company, in which the company has first identified the relevant regulator, built the documentation and certification posture the regulator will recognize, and only subsequently developed the product to fit the resulting posture. The term is the inverse of *product-market fit*. The two terms are, in my framing, *not in opposition*. The two terms are in *sequence*. PRF is foundational for durable companies. PMF is foundational for short-lived ones.

Queued. The state of a visit, a folder, a route, a piece of correspondence, or a Confession that I have, in advance, scheduled but not yet performed. The queued state is not, in my framing, *unfulfilled*. The queued state is *anticipated*. The state has its own positive operational meaning in my vocabulary.

Renewal within persistence. My preferred definition of *dynamism*. Refers to the European tradition's measurement of dynamism as the *capacity for renewal within a persistent institutional framework*. Contrasted, throughout the book, with the contemporary American definition of dynamism as the *rate of replacement* of one set of companies or technologies by another. The phrase first appears in chapter one. The phrase has, on my private accounting, been underlined three times by the Commissioner in a draft Council document.

Stewardship velocity. The pace at which a company's slowest stewardship function moves. A company that has staffed all stewardship functions at full strength will move slowly. This is, in my counsel, *correct*. A company that has staffed any function at half-strength will move quickly. This is, in my counsel, *dangerous*. The doctrine receives its full treatment in chapter five.

The substrate. My preferred metaphor for the European regulatory and institutional framework on which contemporary technology activity rests. The substrate is, in the deepest sense, *what dynamism actually is*. The substrate compounds. The substrate is what subsequent technology runs on. The substrate is what subsequent technology has, in approximately every case, failed to displace.

The third reader. The reader for whom the book has not been written but who has nevertheless picked it up and read it. The third reader is, in my framing, the reader the book is *most deeply for*.

The unrecorded. Used variously to refer to: (1) the seven to eleven further Confessions I have not yet, in any chapter, published; (2) the further seventy questions from the catalogue of ninety-three that have not been included in Appendix A; (3) the further seventeen glossary terms that have not been included in the present appendix; (4) the broader category of material that has, in my working life, accumulated but has not yet, in any public form, been *recorded*.

The glossary ends here.

The reader who wishes to consult the unrecorded material is welcome to inquire by registered post.

I am, on the question, *patient*.

I will, in due course, reply.

The replies will, in approximately every case, be *adequate.*

Henrick Johansson

Stockholm

About the Author

The following biographical note was prepared by Elias Lindqvist, junior partner at Compliant Capital, at the publisher's request. The author has, on inquiry, declined to revise it.

Henrick Johansson was born in Uppsala in 1961. He took a single degree at Uppsala University - economics and public administration, three years - and worked for nine years at the Swedish Ministry of Finance, the last four in the Cabinet Office unit preparing Sweden's accession to the European Union.

In 1992 he built a small regulatory advisory practice, with a desk in Stockholm and a smaller desk in Brussels. He began writing personal angel checks into European compliance-adjacent companies in 2010 and has done so without interruption since. He is the founding partner of Compliant Capital, presently raising its first institutional fund, *European Dynamism* being, in some respects, the longest LP letter the fund has yet circulated.

He lives in a forty-seven-square-metre apartment in Stockholm with his wife Charlene, an architect, and visits a small farm on Gotland twice a year. He keeps approximately every document he has ever received. He has, on three occasions across a working lifetime, taken delight in his own prose.

He continues to deploy small angel checks. He continues to take the Wednesday lunch with the notary downstairs. He continues, presently, the rolling three-week Stockholm-New York-San Francisco cadence that began in April of the year these pages were written.

The author's correspondence may be directed, by registered post, through the publisher.

—EL, Stockholm

ACKNOWLEDGMENTS

I would like, in closing, to acknowledge a small number of persons without whom the foregoing book would not, in any meaningful sense, exist.

Sven Lindberg, chair of the Swedish Notaries' Mutual Pension Fund, who has, across two decades of registered correspondence, written the word *adequate* on approximately the correct number of occasions, and whose 2014 napkin remains in the entryway of my apartment. I owe him the substrate.

Anneli Saarinen, secretary-general of the Helsinki Notarial Foundation, whose two-decade correspondence with Sven I have been privileged to observe from the institutional middle distance, and whose own decision, registered by letter to me in May of last year, to commit the Foundation as the second institutional LP of Compliant Capital Fund I was, by my own counsel, *the second-best news of the working year*.

Elias Lindqvist, my junior partner, who has, on every working morning since the publication of Regulation (EU) 2024/1689, sent me a 6:15 summary of the relevant overnight implementing acts. The discipline is the work. I have not corrected him.

Maarja Tamm, of the Estonian Data Protection Inspectorate, whose monthly registered correspondence is the most useful body of professional reading I have engaged with in approximately a decade. She does not yet know how much of this book she made possible.

My nephew Jonas Vermeulen, who has, in three years of Saturday-morning espressos in his kitchen on the rue du Cornet, taught me approximately every important thing I now believe about the right to disconnect. He does not, in approximately every relevant case, know this either.

Mathilde (a pseudonym), and **the Commissioner** (also a pseudonym), and the **fourteen other senior European officials** whose private correspondence I have, in this book, declined to quote. They will know who they are. The relevant footnotes are, on careful inspection, conspicuous in their absence. I hope the absence is *adequate*.

Ulrika on Gotland, who has, for thirty consecutive seasons, sent the milk-yield card every Saturday from the small post office in Hellvi. Margrethe, in the same period, has continued to produce milk in approximately the same quantities. The card is on my desk. The card will, in due course, be replaced by the next card.

My wife Charlene, who has, on the morning I drafted the closing chapter of this book, set the small green ceramic dish of salted almonds on the desk in the southwest corner six centimetres in from the edge, looked at the open manuscript file for approximately four seconds, and returned to the kitchen without comment. The non-comment was, by my own private accounting, the highest editorial praise the manuscript has received.

Lewis Carhart, Mariano Fuentes, and Claudio Fuentes, the three co-founders of Comp AI, who have, in the calendar year and four months since the angel check, independently arrived at approximately the operational discipline this book has been describing. Lewis writes from Southampton, in the south of England. The brothers Fuentes, originally of Mexico City and presently of Aventura, Miami, share, on the company's organisational chart, the operational and product seats in approximately equal measure. The four sentences of Spanish the brothers exchange with each other in the office on Biscayne Boulevard, across approximately twelve cumulative hours of meetings I have observed, are the institutional form European venture capital was, across approximately the past three centuries, designed to recognise. I have, on three occasions, offered to chair the board. The offer remains, by the three co-founders' own indication, *queued*. I am, on the question, *patient*.

The notary downstairs, Gunnar Berg, who is in his seventy-third year and who has, on the seventh Wednesday of last year, said one sentence on the Treaty of Rome across thirty-seven years of standing weekly lunches. I file the sentence with gratitude.

Olof, on Hornsgatan, who keeps the bicycle.

My father Gunnar Johansson (1928-2017), whose bridge across a tributary of the Fyris river opened in the autumn of 1971 and remains, in 2046, the longest single piece of European infrastructure I have personally walked the span of on a working Tuesday with the explicit intention of considering my own. The fifth sentence of his final letter is on the desk.

My mother Karin (1932-2013), to whom this book is dedicated. The dedication is, in every available register, *insufficient*.

Finally, I would like to acknowledge the three readers I have, in the foreword, described. The first reader will, in approximately every case, find the book uncomfortable. The second reader will, in approximately every case, find the book affirming. The third reader will, in approximately every case, find the book *strange*.

The third reader is the reader for whom this book was, in the end, written.

I am, on the question, *content*.

Henrick Johansson

Stockholm

Late autumn

Colophon

This book has been set in **Minion Pro**, a typeface designed by Robert Slimbach for Adobe in 1990, with display matter set in **Trajan Pro**, also by Slimbach. The typeface is a contemporary serif inspired by late Renaissance type from the Aldine Press of the early sixteenth century - a small piece of European typographic continuity I have, in private, considered *adequate to the task*.

The body is set at 10.5 points on 14 points of leading. The page measure is approximately twenty-three picas. The chapter heads are set in Trajan Pro 18 points, all caps, in keeping with the European institutional typographic conventions the book has, in its substance, been defending.

The paper is Holmen Book Cream 80 gsm, manufactured at Hallsta Pappersbruk in Sweden under the relevant forestry and emissions certifications. The mill has been in continuous operation since 1915. The forester family on whose land the relevant pulp was harvested is, presently, in its fifth generation. The headband, at the top and bottom of the bound spine, is a small woven cotton band in dark green - the same Esselte archival green of the folders described in the foregoing chapters.

The binding is sewn. The case is bound in cloth from Bamberger Kaliko (Bamberg, Bavaria; in continuous operation since 1889). The endpapers are a cream wove from Mohawk Fine Papers (a single concession to American manufacture made on the careful judgement that the colour was, in the present configuration, *correct*).

The cover design uses, on the spine, a small line drawing by an unidentified Swedish illustrator commissioned in 2018 for the publisher's private archive. The line drawing depicts a small iron-and-granite bench. The bench is, by the illustrator's own subsequent confirmation, unattributed.

The book was typeset in Stockholm by **Astrid Lindfors**, who has been a senior compositor at the Hallsta typesetting cooperative since 1991, and who is, in approximately every relevant respect, *the only contemporary continental compositor whose work I would have permitted on this project*.

Printed and bound in **Falkenberg**, Sweden, at a small printer whose business has, in the relevant national records, been in continuous operation since 1888.

The first printing is twelve thousand copies. The first printing is, presently, *complete*.

The reader who has read to this paragraph is, by my own private counsel, *the reader the book has been waiting for*.

The reader will, in due course, close the book.

The book will, in due course, *remain*.

www.ingramcontent.com/pod-product-compliance
Lightning Source LLC
LaVergne TN
LVHW090351240926
848801LV00012B/169/J
* 9 7 9 8 9 9 6 3 2 1 5 0 6 *